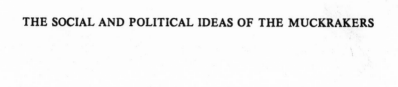

THE SOCIAL AND POLITICAL IDEAS OF THE MUCKRAKERS

"The men with the muckrakes
are often indispensable to the well-being of society;
but only if they know when to stop
raking the muck,
and to look upward to the celestial crown above them,
to the crown of worthy endeavor."

THEODORE ROOSEVELT

The Social
and Political
Ideas of
THE MUCKRAKERS

by DAVID MARK CHALMERS

AYER COMPANY, PUBLISHERS, INC.
SALEM, NEW HAMPSHIRE 03079

Reprint Edition 1984
AYER Company, Publishers, Inc.
47 Pelham Road
Salem, New Hampshire 03079

*In memory of Henry Chalmers,
a dedicated public official
who served the people*

INTERNATIONAL STANDARD BOOK NUMBER:

0-8369-1745-6

LIBRARY OF CONGRESS CATALOG CARD NUMBER:

70-117765

PRINTED IN THE UNITED STATES OF AMERICA

CONTENTS

PREFACE

During the first decade of the twentieth century, a group of magazine journalists educated the American people about the widespread corruption that had attended the growth of industrialism. These "muckrakers" have been amply credited with laying the groundwork for many of the reforms that followed. At the same time the journalists have been generally categorized as either shallow moralists who told "bad" men to be "good," or seekers of scandal whose only interest was in selling magazines.

Those who have written about the muckrakers have usually read only selected articles or studied the topics on which the journalists wrote. This book utilizes the inductive approach, and traces the entire muckrake writings of the major journalists of exposure. The result reaches beyond the familiar depiction of widespread corruption to show the common agreement among the muckrakers as to the cause of the trouble. In addition, this book presents the reform solutions—sometimes shallow, sometimes deep—which each of the muckrakers came to present in his writings, solutions which ranged from the release of business from restrictive halters to the espousal of legislative regulation and socialism.

This study also raises question about the "revisionist" interpretation of the Progressive Era, by showing that the muckrakers were not motivated by Jeffersonian longings, anti-urban and anti-labor prejudices, Anglo-Saxon predilections, racism, or a decline in their own class status.

In limiting this examination to those magazine journalists who specifically made their living by writing detailed stories of graft and corruption, many important participants in the muckrake movement have been necessarily left out. However, the thirteen writers studied here were the core of the movement, and they flooded the popular periodicals with muckrake articles. Although the some six hundred articles and ninety books and reprints of these muckrakers were the basic source for this book, the Ray Stannard Baker, Albert J. Beveridge, Theodore Roosevelt, Charles Edward Russell, and William Allen White Manuscript Collections at the Library of Congress, Washington, D. C., the Ida Tarbell Collection at Allegheny College, Meadville, Pennsylvania, and the Lincoln Steffens Papers at the Columbia University Library, New York City, have been examined. There has been increasing interest in the muckrakers and the Progressive Era, and special note should be taken of Louis Filler's brilliant classic, *Crusaders for American Liberalism*, and Arthur and Lila Weinberg's selection of the journalists' writings in *The Muckrakers*.

Portions of this study published previously in the *Journal of the History of Ideas* and *The American Journal of Economics and Sociology* are used with the kind permission of the editors. I would also like to express appreciation for aid given me by Professor Richard C. Wade, the history faculty of the University of Rochester, Professor Michael Kraus of the City University of New York, Professor George Anderson and the University of Kansas Conference on the Progressive Era, Katherine Brand and the Library of Congress, Professors Arthur W. Thompson, Lyle N. McAlister, Clifton W. Yearly, and Francis C. Haber of the University of Florida, and to Judith Lynn Chalmers, Sallie K. Chalmers, and my wife Jean.

DAVID MARK CHALMERS

Gainesville, Florida

❧ 1 ❧

THE AGE OF THE MUCKRAKE

The reform impulse in America has come from all parts of society. It has not been the exclusive possession of philosophers, middle class reformers, or proletarian organizers and revolutionists. Almost every group in the economy has at one time taken part, and in each generation new leaders have arisen to lead the continuing crusade for social progress. The drive has come from idealistic Virginia planters, Jacksonian farmers and workingmen alarmed over money power, transcendental poets and utopians, humanitarian reformers and educators, New England aristocrats and clergymen opposed to chattel slavery, professional New York politicians who believed in a "higher law" than the Constitution, Radical Republican spoilsmen genuinely concerned with helping the freedmen, influential editors with bulging satchels of remedies, disturbed patricians and respectable businessmen distressed by boodle and the tariff, aroused farmers battling the railroads and monopolies, Greenbackers, Bellamy Nationalists and Single Taxers. In the first decade of the twentieth century, a new voice was added. It came from the writers for the popular magazines, to whom Theodore Roosevelt gave the lasting name "muckrakers."

The important factors in the rise of the muckrakers were the tremendous economic changes which they described, and the growth of the cheap magazines in which they wrote. A revolutionary expansion of the American economy had taken place since the Civil War. While the size of the population and the value of agriculture tripled, the worth of manufactures increased eleven times. The predominant economic philosophy assumed that free competition would keep prices down, prevent the concentration of economic power, and bring steady national improvement and progress. Yet, while the fruits of the great American development gathered in the mouth of the cornucopia, their distribution seemed to have been made through the narrow portion of the horn.

For the farmer something was very wrong. The tariffs, monopolies, railroads, and banks seemed joined together to raise the price of everything he had to buy, while he was forced to sell his own product in a competitive, fluctuating market. Progress seemed to be passing him by. The urban laborer, too, received only a limited share of the new prosperity. Wages rose slowly. Hours were long, and the accident rate climbed. Depressions seemed to come more often and lasted longer, making unemployment a constant threat. The Fourteenth Amendment and a conservative judiciary safeguarded business from effective regulation, and the high protective tariff did its best to prevent foreign competition. In the last decade of the century a financial revolution overlaid the industrial one, bringing further concentration of power. Despite the passage of a federal anti-trust law in 1890, almost all of the major industrial products, and a surprising number of the lesser ones, were being produced under monopolistic conditions.

Many citizens viewed these developments with increasing alarm. In the 1860's and 1870's a number of states attempted to regulate the railroads. In the next decade the Farmers' Alliances extended the battle. The Populists of the 'nineties, fighting against monopoly, sought to accomplish in Washington what the Granger legislation had failed to do in the state capitals. The reformist writings of Henry George and Edward Bellamy were national best sellers. In 1888 both major parties condemned the trusts in their platforms. Though monopolies had been considered illegal under the common law, twenty-seven States passed laws against them, with fifteen including restrictions in their constitutions. In 1890 the Sherman Act declared that every combination or conspiracy in restraint of trade was illegal. In 1900 an Industrial Commission created by Congress began issuing its reports on trusts and industrial combinations, and more than a hundred articles on the same subject appeared in various periodicals. "A List of Books Relating to the Trusts," compiled by the Library of Congress in 1902, contained almost two hundred titles. An influential segment of the press reflected this concern with the concentration of economic power, and in his first annual message to Congress, Theodore Roosevelt supported the view that the trusts were the first subject of the day.[1]

As railroads and industry expanded in the period after the Civil War, so had the popular magazines. The number of magazines increased. Technological improvements in printing and the increased use of advertising enabled the periodicals to reduce prices and reach out for a larger reading public. During the muckraking era, which lasted from 1903 to about 1912, reform magazines could count upon an average monthly circulation of more than three million. When, on occasion, the *Saturday Evening Post* and the *Ladies' Home Journal* threw their weight onto the scales, the combined number amounted to more than five million copies[2] reaching out for the attention of the twenty million American families.

Exposing corruption was not new. Henry Demarest Lloyd's *Wealth Against Commonwealth* (1894) explored the tangled path of the Standard Oil Company nine years before Ida Tarbell wrote her history for *McClure's*. The novels of Frank Norris and Charles Francis Adams' "A Chapter of Erie" (1869) were written in what was to become the typical muckraking style. Charles Edward Russell thought that Henry George, Jr., should receive the first honors. Ray Stannard Baker and Mark Sullivan presented their own claims, and there were others who would have had reasonable credentials. Exposures of municipal graft and corporate corruption have a long and distinguished pedigree. Cicero, laying bare the corruption of the Roman governor of Sicily, was a muckraker of considerable prowess, and Alfred Henry Lewis claimed that Jesus of Nazareth was a member of the profession.[3] What was new and important was the way in which such writings dominated the American popular magazines for most of the first decade of the twentieth century.

By the early 1900's a number of writers were already exposing municipal and industrial corruption. Their separate efforts became a movement when they discovered that their writing about individual and specific complaints really involved a comprehensive critique of American society. The recognition of muckraking as a social philosophy was the particular achievement of the master impresario of the cheap magazine, S. S. McClure. In an editorial in the January, 1903, *McClure's,* he inaugurated the movement:

"How many of those who have read through this number of the magazine noticed that it contains three articles on one subject? We did not plan it so; it is a coincidence that the January *McClure's* is such an arraignment of American character as should make every one of us stop and think. How many noticed that? . . . Miss Tarbell has our capitalists conspiring among themselves, deliberately, shrewdly, upon legal advice, to break the law so far as it restrained them, and to misuse it to restrain others who were in their way. Mr. Baker shows labor, the ancient enemy of capital, and the chief complainant of the trusts' unlawful acts, itself committing and excusing crimes. And in "The Shame of Minneapolis" we see the administration of a city employing criminals to commit crimes for the profit of the elected officials, while the citizens . . . stood by complacent and not alarmed.

"Capitalists, workingmen, politicians, citizens—all breaking the law, or letting it be broken. Who is left to uphold it? The lawyers? Some of the best lawyers . . . advise corporations and business firms how they can get around the law without too great a risk of punishment. The judges? Too many of them so respect the laws that for some "error" or quibble they restore to office and liberty men convicted on evidence overwhelmingly convincing to common sense. The churches? We know of one, an ancient and wealthy establishment, which had to be compelled . . . to put its tenements in sanitary condition. The colleges? They do not understand.

"There is no one left: none but all of us . . . . We have to pay in the end, every one of us. And in the end the sum total of the debt will be our liberty."[4]

The journalists of exposure, then, were concerned with much more than the corruption of public officials or the illegal activities of corporations. They described a condition in which all of the individual parts seemed to conspire against the whole of society, each seeking its own benefit at a cost to the rest. This was not, moreover, simply enlightened self-interest at work, for it proceeded in conspiratorial fashion to violate the law and jeopardize free institutions. The muckrakers seemed to be explaining, as McClure pointed out, the moral disintegration of a whole society.

In a speech delivered in 1906 at the laying of the cornerstone of the House of Representatives Office Building, President Theodore Roosevelt excoriated the movement and gave it a name. "In Bunyan's 'Pilgrim's Progress,' " he stated, "you may recall the description of the Man with the Muck-rake, the man who could look no way but downward, with the muck-rake in his hand; who was offered a celestial crown for his muck-rake, but who would neither look up nor regard the crown he was offered, but continued to rake to himself the filth on the floor."

The journalists to whom he thus gave the collective title of "muckrakers" did go in for sensationalism. In some cases they deliberately set out, as one of them later put it, to "find shame," and in other instances publishers encouraged exposés solely to stimulate circulation.[5] They made use of bold print, startling titles, and eye-catching covers. They often wrote fervent denunciations with exaggerated adjectives, taking advantage of what Walter Lippmann has described as the distinct American prejudice in favor of those who make accusations.[6] Perhaps it was the combination of factual detail and emotion that contributed much to their success. Despite the flamboyant trappings of their trade, however, the muckrakers were much too concerned with the seriousness of their purpose to jeopardize it by false or unsubstantiated charges. Since they specifically named names and places, they could have been destroyed in the courts if they had not been careful of their facts. Most of their information came from court records and Congressional investigations. They did not uncover corruption—although there were notable original exposures—as much as they brought before the public eye the mountainous details of graft which crowded the public records.

Far from seeking to tear down, the muckrakers labored for the definite purpose of social betterment. Though they differed among themselves as to the nature of the changes they sought, they were nevertheless united by a common body of discovery and analysis which gave continuity and substance to muckraking as a social philosophy. No matter where they went and of what they wrote, they found that business and the big businessman were busily engaged in corruption. Public opinion had deified the search for wealth, and in this new religion the tycoon had become the high priest. He received his permit for corruption from the citizens themselves who had been corrupted by adulation of wealth and business success. Times and conditions had changed without a concomitant alteration in law and morals. The eighteenth century's legal structure was appropriate only for a free competitive system unassailed by aggregates of economic wealth and power. Vast new concentrations found themselves constricted by the outdated framework and refused to be contained. Instead they sought their own direction and broke down every obstacle in their path. "The crux of muckraking," the chief historian of the movement, Louis Filler, has written, "was the realistic analysis of the deeper maladjustments of society."[7] Whatever their particular solutions were, the muckrakers sought to bring the economic mechanism of the nation back into balance by seeking a role of social responsibility for business.

The muckrakers, then, were the school of magazine journalists of the first decade of the twentieth century who wrote factual accounts of the widespread corruption of society by the forces of wealth. They showed the source of this evil to be the clash between the new economic development and the old laws and organization of society. The people, hypnotized by wealth, permitted the systematic corruption of all of the instrumentalities of government and public opinion by a new ruling class—the businessmen.

In the decade between 1903 and 1912, nearly two thousand articles of a muckraking variety appeared in the popular magazines, complemented by editorials, cartoons, and serials. These articles were written by journalists, college professors, reformers, conservationists, ministers, and public officials. But of this vast outpouring, close to a third were written by a small group of twelve men and one woman who concentrated on and professionalized this kind of journalism. They constituted the heart of the muckraking movement. They were able writers of varied experience, and each carved out a niche in which he became a recognized authority.

SAMUEL HOPKINS ADAMS was a graduate of Hamilton College, Clinton, New York, and came to *Collier's Weekly* from the *New York Sun* and *McClure's*. Adams centered his attention on health, the struggle against disease, and a campaign against fraudulent patent medicines.

RAY STANNARD BAKER studied at Michigan State and the University of Michigan before becoming a newspaper reporter in Chicago. During his career as a muckraker with *McClure's* and the *American Magazine,* he reported on the railroads, labor, the color question in the North and South, and the impact of the new economic conditions on the churches. Under the pseudonym of David Grayson, he authored an extremely successful series of reflections on rural life, "Adventures in Contentment."

CHRISTOPHER P. CONNOLLY was prosecuting attorney of Butte, Montana, during the days of the political battles of the copper kings. He wrote a history of Montana for *McClure's* and covered the celebrated Haywood-Moyer and McNamara labor-violence trials. In 1909 he conducted the *Collier's* campaign for conservation against Interior Secretary Ballinger and the Taft Administration. His major concern was relationship between the judiciary and Big Business.

BURTON J. HENDRICK received his master's degree from Yale while an editor of the New Haven *Morning News*. During his eight years with *McClure's,* before he became an associate editor of *World's Work,* Hendrick exposed the activities of the life insurance companies and described the building of a number of the great New York fortunes.

WILL IRWIN left Stanford University for the life of a reporter on Pacific Coast newspapers before going East to the New York *Sun*. He wrote of racial unrest in the West, the saloon, and a series on American newspapers for *Collier's*.

THOMAS W. LAWSON, a Bostonian, was a prominent broker, financier and tempestuous manipulator on the New York Stock Exchange. When he fell out with the Standard Oil interests, the editors of *Everybody's* asked him to "tell all" in their magazine. The result was "Frenzied Finance, the Story of Amalgamated Copper."

ALFRED HENRY LEWIS had moved west from Cleveland, been a rancher, lawyer, and then a newspaperman in Kansas City. He went to Washington for the *Chicago News* and later as head of William Randolph Hearst's Washington Bureau. Lewis was one of the most prolific writers among the muckrakers. A self-styled individualist, intimate of Tammany, and a prowler of the streets of New York, Lewis wrote about the dominant individuals in a golden age of finance.

DAVID GRAHAM PHILLIPS grew up in Indiana and was educated at De Pauw and Princeton. He moved upward from reporting in Cincinnati to become London correspondent for Joseph Pulitzer's New York *World*. He "muckraked" primarily for Hearst's *Cosmopolitan,* for which he wrote a sensational series on "Treason of the Senate." In addition, he turned out twenty-six novels, often on muckrake themes.

CHARLES EDWARD RUSSELL was associated with most of the reform movements of his lifetime: Single Tax, Free Trade, Greenback, Populist, Muckrake, and Socialist. He was city editor of the New York *World,* managing editor of the New York *American,* and publisher of the Chicago *American.* Lured from his study of literature to do an expose of the beef trust for *Everybody's,* Russell was soon turning out more articles on more subjects than any of the other muckrakers.

UPTON SINCLAIR found an early home in the Socialist Party. Never a professional journalist, he broke into the magazine columns as a contributor by virtue of having become prominent as a Socialist and the creator of the muckrake classic, *The Jungle.*

LINCOLN STEFFENS attended the University of California before setting off on a grand tour of European universities. An intimate of Theodore Roosevelt, he came to number business-

men, grafters, bosses, politicians, radicals, and reformers among
his friends. In order to provide an example of what an aroused
civic spirit could accomplish, he tried to reform a whole city,
and in an attempt to apply his philosophy of practical Christianity, he became involved in the labor-violence trial of the
McNamara brothers. Steffens' best-known writings were investigations of the corruption of municipal and state governments.

IDA M. TARBELL, a daughter of the Pennsylvania oil regions,
was educated at Allegheny College and had been an editor of
The Chautauquan before going to the Sorbonne to study and
write history. When she returned from genteel poverty in Paris,
S. S. McClure set her to work on a life of Abraham Lincoln.
She wrote her famous "History of the Standard Oil Company"
for *McClure's* and made studies of the tariff and of the American woman for the *American Magazine*.

GEORGE KIBBE TURNER graduated from Williams College, and
worked as a newspaperman for fifteen years before becoming
the *McClure's* expert on municipal government. He wrote on
the liquor traffic, the white slave trade and prostitution, and won
special attention with his article 'The Daughters of the Poor."

There were many others who wrote muckraking articles and
who could not be omitted from a complete list of the muckrakers. Men such as William Bayard Hale, Samuel E. Mof-
fett, C. M. Keys, and Mark Sullivan made substantial contributions, but they were primarily financial or political colum-
nists and might legitimately be separated from the core group.
S. S. McClure, B. O. Flower of the *Arena* and *Twentieth
Century*, and Norman Hapgood of *Collier's* did much writing
themselves. They suggested many of the best topics and generally attempted to channel the movement, but they were more
editors than muckrake writers. Others like William Hard
and Isaac Marcosson produced exposés, but did so as sidelines
to more generalized journalistic careers. John Mathews wrote

about graft but only when his pet subjects of water power and conservation were involved. Josiah Flynt, Finley Peter Dunn, and William Allen White offered contributions too individual and in style too personalized to be considered primarily as muckraking. The writings of Gustavus Myers seldom appeared in the magazines. All of these people, and more, added to the agitation and shared in the enthusiasm. They were an important part of the movement, but if they approached the core, they were not of it.

The muckrakers worked together on a variety of newspapers and magazines, and thought of themselves as bound together in striving for the common betterment. Samuel Hopkins Adams met Will Irwin while on an assignment on the West Coast and brought him to the New York *Sun.* It was on that training ground of reform-minded journalists that Irwin came to know David Graham Phillips. When Phillips moved on to the New York *World,* he came under the special protection of its city editor, Charles Edward Russell. When Phillips' "The Treason of the Senate" brought Theodore Roosevelt's wrath down upon the journalists of exposure, the beleaguered author turned to Russell for comfort. Alfred Henry Lewis tried to act as a peacemaker between Phillips and the President, and it was to Lewis that Phillips turned when he wished to learn about poverty and crime in New York City.[8] When, in 1908, Russell decided to join the Socialist Party, Phillips pleaded tearfully against it. Steffens questioned the wisdom of Russell's action, and Alfred Henry Lewis denounced "such foolishness" with a vehemence so strong that Russell remembered it vividly almost thirty years later. But he continued to be a member of the circle in the backroom of Considine's Saloon on Broadway near 42nd Street, where Lewis held daily court.[9] Steffens, the old master at friendships, knew them all. He was President of the Liberal Club on East 19th Street, which catered to writers of the socialist and reform variety. Russell was Vice-President and Ray

Stannard Baker one of the members. Steffens and Baker also belonged to Robert Hunter's luncheon discussion circle that met at Luchow's Resturant every Wednesday.[10] Steffens was one of "the McClure's group" and worked with Baker, Irwin, Ida Tarbell, Burton Hendrick, and C. P. Connolly. Disagreeing with the editor's speculative schemes, the cream of the *McClure's* organization, led by Steffens, Tarbell and Baker, left to bring out their own *American Magazine*.

Muckraking was, then, a movement by association as well as identity of purpose. Its members were people of experience and affairs. They wrote ably and with spirit, and they attracted wide public attention.

❧ 2 ❧

SALVATION THROUGH BIG BUSINESS:

GEORGE KIBBE TURNER

Bad government was not new to America, but by the twentieth century it had become an increasingly serious problem. The rapid growth of population and the industrialization and urbanization of the nation added to the difficulties of city and state administration. The standard solution to municipal corruption was "business government" with the politicians replaced by the leaders of trade and industry. There was a certain validity to this point of view. In the post-Civil War era many of the ablest men shunned politics to devote themselves to the accumulation of wealth. There was a widespread popular conviction that if these successful men would turn their hand to public affairs —'even temporarily — dishonest administration would be ended. Most of the muckrakers disagreed for they came to believe that business morality was itself the greatest enemy to orderly government.

Only George Kibbe Turner took the traditional view. All of the standard components were there: vice, bribery, boodle, franchises, municipal service corporations, vested interests, business, bigness, and public apathy. Turner saw that the economic organization of the nation had changed greatly without an equal change in institutions and attitudes. The result was greed and lawlessness. In an early short story and novel he had tested out the hypothesis that "business" was at fault [1] but by the time that he joined company with the muckrakers for *McClure's* in 1906, he had forsaken his earlier view. Instead of a profit-manipulated and corrupted society, he saw an experimentally progressing one. Beginning with the rebuilding of storm-devastated Galveston, he studied municipal conditions and reform in Chicago, New York, Boston, Des Moines and Cincinnati. His description of what happened in Galveston was without complication. Corruption had been the result of an alliance between crooked politics and vice, but the institution of efficient commission government operated by businessmen on a businesslike basis ended all this. [2]

When Lincoln Steffens left *McClure's* in 1906, Turner became the magazine's expert on municipal affairs, developing the contrasting themes of political corruption and business salvation. There were, he maintained, two chief exploiters of American cities: the public service corporations, and the forces of liquor, crime, and vice. The first engaged in robbery by illegally "buying" franchises, and the second existed by purchasing protection from the police. The corporations, however, did not organize this civic wrong-doing; they only made an incidental contribution to it. With this casual comment, Turner dismissed their role from his analysis and went on to deal with what he considered to be the "older and more basic evil." [3] Thereafter, when he wrote of the widespread nature of corruption and "the interests" which developed from the despoliation of the law, he meant only the activities of organized vice.

The liquor interests were the greatest menace, for they were responsible for bossism, ward control, purchase of police, outbreaks of theft, robbery, crimes of violence, gambling, dope, and prostitution. It was a world of commercialized savagery. America was saturated with saloons. The brewers, who were the great power among the liquor interests, created a competition so keen that the saloons could not make a profit through honest operation. To operate successfully, which almost inevitably meant illegally, they had to buy immunity from the law. Of all the vice which alcohol engendered and encouraged, the worst was the white slave trade, and Turner became a recognized authority on that "social question." He wrote articles on the operation of the various systems that preyed upon the "daughters of the poor," and testified at official investigations.[4]

In singling out the growing city as a distinctive facet of American life, Turner dealt with it not only as a center of machine-controlled corruption, but also as a testing ground for civic action. Although he emphasized its shady role ("from scarlet Babylon to smoky Chicago . . . the great market place of dissipation"),[5] he was also concerned with the city as a place to work out the social adjustments which national change and growth were making necessary. Turner wrote of the city as primarily a business body, a great cooperative association for the transaction of community affairs. The citizen was a "corporator" and the handling of urban problems served as a model for the whole nation.[6] This use of commercial phraseology to describe urban life was no accident in the writing of a man who found municipal salvation stemming from the business community. Whereas Lincoln Steffens and the other muckrakers found that betterment grew from convincing the businessman to reverse his ethic, Turner encouraged its spread.

Turner carried through his theme of salvation by business with considerable fidelity. In writing on the question "Shall the Mineral Wealth of Alaska Enrich the Guggenheim Trust or the United States Treasury?" he showed that the American people ended up paying monopoly prices for what had been their own property. What was the answer? The resources of public lands had eventually to be developed by corporations, yet most of the laws of the United States recognized only in-dividuals. The corporations were thus forced to turn to fraud. Turner's solution was to establish a "modern" procedure that would benefit everyone, with the public receiving its share by some sort of undefined regulation or taxation. Perhaps, the public interest would be decided by enlightened business, which was the hero of Turner's articles. "Modern government," he wrote, "is more and more devoted to economic questions; it is business speaking in the largest and best sense of the term."[7]

This was his underlying message in "The Masters of Capital in America" which he wrote with the trust expert John Moody.[8] Telling the industrial and financial history of the United States since the Civil War, Turner expressed fear of the dangers of the centripetal nature of great wealth. However, he leveled his most forceful attack against what he termed the outmoded, ruinous concept of competition. He seldom mentioned regula-tion and never described it; public ownership he dismissed as impractical. While the explicit theme of "The Masters of Capital in America" was the power that wealth was placing in the hands of a few, the implicit argument was much more in keeping with Turner's previously expressed ideas. As if to counterbalance the traditional objections, he eulogized the sense of responsibility of the great magnates. Huge combina-tions were inevitable and necessary to prevent the wastefulness of competition and to rationalize business.

J. P. Morgan, he explained, was fighting for the real in-vestors who for more than twenty years had watched the disastrous manipulation of their properties result in crises such as the "terrible American panic" of 1893. "In the United States, where every tradition has tended toward the most ex-treme type of individualism, the concentration of capital in the form of monopoly is probably more actively hated and resisted than in any other portion of the globe," he explained. "Yet, from the standpoint of modern capital, monopoly is absolutely and irresistibly logical. . . . The effort to secure monopoly in modern industry is nothing more than the effort of capital to secure just the amount of investment in machinery which will produce the greatest possible returns. What could be more vicious than the waste of the savings of the race in the duplication of machinery which it does not need to do its work? What a wild, crazy, wasteful thing, to build two railroads where one ought to run! In American railroads the capital of the world was being wasted by tens of millions, and there was no sign of relief."[9] The achievement of J. P. Morgan was that he had placed industry beyond the reach of fluctuations, raids, and the petty manipulations of irresponsible wealth. He had built "a corporation too large to be bought."[10]

Although G. K. Turner criticized as outdated the statutes governing corporate activity, he gave no more than passing attention to the role of the law as a factor in the national corruption. The most revealing study of the judicial process and institutions was made by a lawyer-turned-muckraker, Christopher P. Connolly.

❧ 3 ❧

THE LAW:

CHRISTOPHER POWELL CONNOLLY

The existence of a "good" law on the statute books does not necessarily mean the achievement of justice. Much more often this depends on what the government and the courts do with the law. In their practical effect, the Interstate Commerce and Sherman Acts functioned as public palliatives rather than effective cures in the early years of the twentieth century. Grover Cleveland's Attorney General, Richard Olney, had pointed out the effect of the "paper existence" of laws. Advising a railroad president against seeking the abolition of the Interstate Commerce Commission, he stated that "the Commission, as its functions have now been limited by the courts, is, or can be made, of great use to the railroads. It satisfies the popular clamor for government supervision of the railroads at the same time that that supervision is almost entirely nominal."[1]

Judges were usually chosen from among successful members of the bar. Their training, income, business associations, and social position influenced them toward conservatism in social ideas and the special defense of wealth in their legal concepts. While the courts tended to guarantee only the procedural rights of individuals, they extended substantive protection to property. In 1875, Supreme Court Justice Samuel F. Miller commented that "it is vain to contend with judges who have been at the Bar the advocates for forty years of railroad companies, and all the forms of associated capital, when they were called upon to decide cases where such interests are in contest. All their training, all their feelings are from the start in favor of those who need no such influence."[2] The journalist of exposure gave considerable attention to this problem, but it took a muckraker with a legal background to make the most important contribution to the understanding of abuses in the judicial system.

Christopher P. Connolly's first offering to the world of popular journalism was "The Story of Montana." It was a tale that he was particularly well qualified to tell. As a businessman, lawyer, and finally prosecuting attorney of Butte, he had been on the scene of many of the episodes which he described.[3] He began with an early history of Montana, which he pictured as a struggle for law and order. The end to lawlessness finally came in the form of vigilante action, which Connolly tended to support as unhappy but necessary. However, the narrative, and indeed the State of Montana, seemed to be marking time until the discovery of copper. With it came the rise of men such as Marcus Daly and William A. Clark, the copper kings of Montana.

When Clark sought election to the United States Senate, the contending forces joined battle in "one of the most corrupt political and commercial conflicts known to history. This struggle between mining kings of limitless wealth made hundreds of men, and ruined thousands; it perverted the moral sense of entire communities; it placed scores of prominent men within the shadow of prison-walls; it destroyed promising political careers, and checked worthy names from the scroll of state and national fame."[4] Held in almost hypnotic fascination,

Connolly detailed the growing orgy of corruption and the pressures which no one seemed able to escape. But for all of its spectacle, Connolly's account was thin because he offered no description of the social and economic factors conditioning the conflict. There is something unreal about Connolly's picture of this struggle of titans who had risen from nowhere to engage in a herculean struggle for a position of unexplained value, through the expenditure of millions of dollars whose origin was only that it "came from copper."

In his subsequent writing, Connolly filled in the background and gave meaning to the activities and events he described. The new factor that made this possible was his discovery of the corporation. The history of American lawlessness, he came to argue, consisted primarily not of the monumental debaucheries of power-mad individuals such as he had known in Montana, but rather of the persistent, day-to-day conniving and corruption practiced by business interests. As a lawyer and a Westerner, Connolly found an ample field in which he could wield a muckrake with special competence.

Because of his legal experience and his knowledge of the West, *Collier's* sent him to report the murder trials of two sets of Western labor leaders. Covering the Moyer-Haywood trial in Idaho, he castigated the lawlessness of the Western Federation of Miners. It was, he maintained, more interested in building a fighting force to "strike terror to the heart of capitalism" than in promoting by "just and fair means the real interests of labor." In the end, he felt, the accused labor leaders were fortunate to have been able to escape through holes in the judicial system. Writing four years later, in 1911, on the trial of the dynamiters of the Los Angeles *Times* building, he seemed very favorably inclined toward the McNamaras themselves. However, with his habitual distaste for doctrinaire beliefs and radical systems, he opposed the Socialist drive for power in Los Angeles. He also attacked the defense lawyer

Clarence Darrow, whom he believed clearly guilty of an attempt to bribe one of the jurors.[5]

Although Connolly detailed the crimes, brutality, and bloodshed for which the unions had been responsible, he believed that the rank and file did not support the terrorists. The real core of the labor troubles of the mining regions stemmed from the actions of "the interests." The worst conditions prevailed in Colorado, where continuing strife kept enmity alive everywhere. The power of capital to use Federal troops and militia, the legislature, and the courts, to conduct campaigns of terror against labor "prodded men, ordinarily law-abiding, to anger and violence." This was the source of the chronic labor conflict of the West. "If wealth could be curbed in its injustice," Connolly maintained, "I believe labor would soon abate its own violence. . . . I never felt as much contempt for Haywood as I did for the Smelter trust."[6]

In the years between 1908 and 1912, Connolly set forth the extent of corporate corruption by describing the behavior of its public representatives. Senator Charles W. Fulton of Oregon had come to power as a member of a notorious machine and had evidenced no sense of public trust. Senator Levi Ankeny of Washington got to the Senate as a vote buyer and was a "political harlequin, used for money-milking purposes by a coterie of lobbyists." Jacob H. Gallinger of New Hampshire was a servant of the Boston and Maine Railroad, rather than the people, and had voted for every grab and against every regulatory act. Senator Francis E. Warren of Wyoming was a failure in business until he went to the Senate and became a millionaire. Billy Barnes and the bosses of Albany did not serve the city, but rather it served them.

In each case Connolly found that the railroads were involved in the corruption. Where they did not cause it, they at least sought a share of the profits. They were everywhere exploiting mineral resources and seeking possession of public lands. In

West Virginia the combination of the coal barons and the Baltimore and Ohio railroad dominated the Legislature. In New Hampshire the Boston and Maine was more potent than the memory of Daniel Webster. The Southern Pacific was the real government of California, for it virtually owned the Legislature and the courts. In addition to preventing regulatory legislation and corrupting public officials, the railroads opposed tariff reform and sought to suppress water commerce. The chief aim of the railroads everywhere was to prevent the rise of competitors who would end the special tax which monopoly enabled them to exact from the necessities of the people.[7]

Such problems were national, Connolly came to believe, because the power of the railroads and corporations was national. The Federal government was a particular target of "the interests" because it possessed the vast and desirable resources of the Western lands. Connolly's major counterattack came in 1909, when he was hired to take charge of the *Collier's* campaign against the Taft Administration's Western land policy. The result was the public explosion of the Ballinger-Pinchot controversy which badly hurt the reputation of the Taft Administration.[8]

Connolly's solution to corporate lawlessness was strongly influenced by his legal background. He believed in competition and felt that the government might be able to check the rampages of the railroads if it made use of the penal provisions of the Interestate Commerce and Sherman Acts.[9] The laws of the nation failed, not because they were basically inadequate, but because they were not being properly carried out. Since democracy was a government by law, it was ultimately controlled by those who made the final interpretation—the courts. Reform of the judiciary was the basic cure for wrong-doing.

The theme of the application of the law was prominent in almost every article. The denial of justice by subservient judges led to continued strife in Colorado. The leaders of the Western

Federation of Miners had gone free in Idaho only because of basic flaws in judicial procedure. Labor violence was bound to continue "as long as Justice is a manikin for capital and a Juggernaut for labor."[10]

Connolly believed that the traditional American regard for the law, and particularly the judicial system, was indeed a factor in the law's corruption. The sacrosanct position of the courts enabled "the interests," when defeated elsewhere, to operate through the judiciary. "Indeed," Connolly phrased it, "the things that are oppressive in the tariff, in freight rates, in financial trusts and industrial monopolies, in private exploitation of public service, and in the seizure of privilege, are in large measure due to the courts' obedience to the will of powerful interests."[11]

The law, which favored the rich, had to be made more equitable. The path was simplification of procedure, ending of delays, and the appointment of men who were less conservative and less likely to put property rights before human rights. Decisions should be shorter and simpler with greater emphasis on the court's logic. Limitation of the power of judicial review would prevent usurpations such as the "rule of reason," by which the courts remade the acts of the legislatures. Since impeachment and recall of judges had proved ineffectual, an experiment might be tried with the recall of the decisions themselves. Publicity and criticism, which Connolly hoped would operate as a check on judicial conservatism, seemed also the means by which his formal changes might be effected.[12] How public opinion, the source of which he had described as being controlled by 'the interests," would function,he did not say.

Whatever the limitations of his approach, Connolly was ably and expertly treating an important aspect of the widespread corruption. He had come to believe that business privilege was the greatest enemy to democracy. He saw the corporations provoking labor violence in Colorado, controlling legislatures in the East, exploiting public lands in the West, and protecting their ill-gotten gains by placing their men in the Senate of the United States. As a lawyer, Connolly believed that the judicial institutions of the nation were basic to all others. By controlling the courts, business was able to do whatever it wished. The re-establishment of governmental honesty and integrity depended on reforming the judiciary. Although the single-mindedness of his philosophy was a weakness as well as strength, Christopher P. Connolly's critical studies of the nature and the course of the law were a vital contribution to the era of the muckrakers.

In suggesting only those reforms which touched upon the law and the judiciary, Connolly never thought to question, or even discuss, the efficacy of the American competitive system. Alfred Henry Lewis, Will Irwin, Burton J. Hendrick, and Ida Tarbell shared his faith in the beneficial workings of competition. Nevertheless, they seemed to believe that a defense of the system was in order, and some of them felt that further corrective measures were necessary to make it work.

❧ 4 ❧

COMPETITION:

ALFRED HENRY LEWIS

AND WILL IRWIN

Those who sought to preserve competition had to begin with
the assumption that their chosen system was not only morally
desirable but economically sound. Competition had, at least
in name, long been the American way. Did not the growth of
monopoly indicate serious and perhaps irreparable weaknesses?
Since the system was considered largely a self-adjusting mechanism, there might be logical difficulty if extensive and continued governmental intervention was necessary to maintain
it. What its supporters could not admit was an evolution beyond the competitive stage. The flaws involved and the evils
that emerged had, of necessity, to be minor in nature. If
anything was wrong, it was because people violated the laws
and were not punished, or because public opinion was being
led momentarily astray, or because some single aspect of the
machine had gotten temporarily out of order.

   Although he called for much in the way of specific governmental action, Alfred Henry Lewis believed that the economy
was essentially sound. He was convinced that the individualistic
instinct was too firmly grounded in man to be overcome perma-
nently by mere concentrated power and wealth. Will Irwin

also escaped dealing with the disturbing question of the possible failure of competition by his vague conception that it was involved in the nature of society itself, and thus free from organized challenge.

Before his appearance in the field of magazine journalism, Alfred Henry Lewis had been a newspaperman and was the author of the Wolfville tales, a series of extremely popular stories of Western individualism.[1] In 1898 he became editor and chief contributor of *The Verdict,* a weekly devoted to the Democratic Party and the political hopes of its publisher, O. H. P. Belmont. For two years he trenchantly attacked the power of the wealthy and demanded reform. When Belmont was not selected for the Vice-Presidency and Bryan was defeated at the polls, *The Verdict* closed down. In a final rambling editorial, Lewis emphasized his usual message that the purity of the individual voter had to be established before politics could be cleansed. With rancor born of disappointment, he lashed out at the masses whom he found were "as treacherous as the classes, and would sell out for less."[2] The era of the muckrakers neither added to nor subtracted from this attitude. As editor of the *Onlooker* and *Human Life,* political columnist for *World Today* (and later when it became *Hearst's Magazine*), and as a regular contributor to the other journals of exposure, he always wrote in the same fashion with the same conclusions.

His specialty was New York politics. It provided him with the material for *The Boss and How He Came to Rule New York, Richard Croker, The Confessions of a Detective, The Diary of a New York Policeman, The Chief, Apaches of New York,* and *Nation-Famous New York Murders.* When David Graham Phillips roamed at night through the streets of New York, collecting material for his masterpiece, *Susan Lenox,* Lewis acted as his guide. In *The Boss and How He Came to Rule New York,* a thinly disguised life of his friend Boss

Croker, Lewis described the old game of taking advantage of the immigrant. Faced with the connection between politics, the police and the courts, the private citizens were powerless. When one of them attempted to protest his rights, he was quickly acquainted with the facts of life: "You're a taxpayer, eh? All right; I'm a ward-leader of Tammany Hall. You're a taxpayer; good! I'm the man that settles how much you pay."[3] Tammany had become all-powerful because everyone—individual, corporation and church—was willing to violate laws in the pursuit of money. The respectable, as well as the politicians, had their price. How could "good government" movements be of any real consequence? The reformers themselves were men of property and affairs and always balked before touching their own interests. They too were caught on the hook of private gain, and they accomplished nothing.

Writing about people, Lewis only rarely turned to the straight analysis of conditions and events. He loved his heroes and hated their enemies. His books on Andrew Jackson, John Paul Jones, and Aaron Burr were romances of triumphant achievement rather than biographies. The story of Aaron Burr, for instance, shows its hero superior to such lesser men as George Washington and the founding fathers. In his articles of exposure, Lewis generally chose the "robber barons" as his subjects. In his rococo style of extravagant hyperbole and classical references, he excoriated the Rockefellers and the Havemeyers, James Stillman, Elihu Root, Boss Platt, and the Senate of the United States.

But what did individualism mean to a world in need of reform? Surely any solution wrought by a few strong men would be the negation of individualism. Lewis lauded Theodore Roosevelt, William Randolph Hearst, and Tom-Lawson as the leaders of the movement against the money criminals,[4] but he was not content to rest his hopes for civilization on a few shoulders, however broad. Essentially, to believe in individualism means relying not on the few but upon all.

Public opinion was the only sure method for the control of wealth, yet it was not functioning because it had been corrupted. The withering scorn Lewis felt for the rich was matched only by that which he directed at their victims. The poor were as thievish, as tyrannical, and, he complained, as mendacious. They wanted riches and wished to tear down the mighty out of sheer envy. The very existence of a billionaire no matter how benevolent, corrupted the public sense of economic values and debauched the popular imagination. The proper function of laws, it seemed, was the removal of corrupting influences from the popular mind. Therefore, although he continued to push for policies such as public ownership of utilities and railroads, Lewis was not much concerned with the details of specific enactments. If one law did not work, then other legislation could be tried until a law was found that accomplished what was wanted.[5] Behind the reform as in all things—once the hindrances were removed—was self-interest. Man was selfish; he was a born competitor. To Lewis, this was his salvation. The bit of the wolf in all men was the health and strength of society. The natural instincts of competition and perpetual discontent were the powerful moving force essential to progress. Any form of collectivism would stifle progress because it would do away with the dynamism of individualistic acquisitiveness.[6]

In a panel discussion with David Graham Phillips and John W. Ghent for *Cosmopolitan*, Lewis flatly laid down his alternative to Socialism. Replying to Ghent, he stated that "for the 'oppression' you speak of, I offer the remedy of manhood and individual independence; for the 'hunger,' work; for the 'graft and swindling,' Sing Sing. There isn't, take it any way you will, an evil named by socialism that an honest thorough enforcement of existing law wouldn't cure. If the law be not enforced, that is the public's fault."[7] Thus the individualism which he prescribed was no gentle palliative but was strong medicine to be rammed down the throat of a malingering public. Alfred Henry Lewis was not a patient man. He had no sympathy for what he considered sham and pretension. The "people" continued to irritate this Western individualist by refusing to fulfil their competitive role.[8]

The most momentous problem for those who believed in the instinctive nature of competition was how to make the many compete better and the few less well. Lewis believed that the latter had been successful because public apathy permitted them special privileges. Economic inequalities, therefore, were the result of a general moral shortcoming, which was in turn created by the popular adulation of wealth. In his journalistic career Lewis attempted to break this invidious circle. Popular complacency had to be upset in order that the people would no longer worship the great fortunes whose very existence had dulled the spirit of individualism. The ingrained competitive instinct needed a great deal of prompting.

To Will Irwin, the competitive instinct did not need stimulation. By the time he came to muckraker councils in 1907, exposure was no longer a startling discovery. Ray Stannard Baker, Lincoln Steffens, and many others stumbled blindly into a world of corruption. The extent of the wrong-doing came like a revelation, and they zealously launched a crusade for correction. By the time of Irwin's entry the movement was a well-defined, profitable, and professional enterprise. This did not mean insincerity on the part of those who came later, but it did lead to a slightly different orientation and emphasis. Having a fair idea of what they would find, the problems they discovered alarmed them less, and their proposed solutions were consequently less drastic in nature.[9]

Will Irwin's first contribution was a series on racial conflict on the Pacific Coast, which he believed was caused by economic competition. The Anglo-Saxon passion for racial purity made it impossible to assimilate other peoples, but no such barrier could restrain economic forces. The able, industrious, and proud Orientals were out-competing the native American. The antagonism which this created, he later wrote, was seized upon by the powerful Harriman interests in California as a stalking-horse for their own activities. A similar rivalry between Negroes and poor whites caused, Irwin believed, racial unrest, and particularly lynching, in the South.[10]

Irwin offered no particular solution to this problem and the interests that fished in its troubled waters. While he condemned the Anglo-Saxon tradition of race antagonism and intolerance, he saw no way in which the Oriental could either be segregated or assimilated. Although he wrote of the position of the Oriental with sympathy and understanding, the answer seemed to be exclusion. The trouble in the South lent itself to no such facile remedy.

Will Irwin's writings on the subject of the Negro had resulted from his research on the growth of the Prohibition movement in America. He saw the liquor question as the result of the widespread connection between vice and the big corporations.[11] In the intricate web of finance and business, the big organizations like the brewers, the Standard Oil Company, and the Southern Pacific Railroad always seemed to stand behind widespread corruption. During his career as a muckraker, Irwin described the operation of this connection in relation to the saloon, the city bosses, and the press.

The saloon historically had been involved in politics as the "poor man's club," and became the base of the political bosses who ruled most American cities. This naturally involved it in graft, corruption, and vice. The growing movement for Prohibition, however, stemmed more directly from the activities of the big brewers. Their demands for exclusive outlets meant the establishment of several taverns in areas which formerly supported one. In order to exist, the owner of each bar literally had to force two drinks down the human gullet where before one had sufficed. In this pursuit of profit for the brewer and a living for the barman, every opportunity for evasion of laws and connection with crime was encouraged.

Despite vague promises and a certain amount of superficial reform, the big interests had no intention of cleaning house. For two generations they rested secure in the belief that they could remain safe through corrupt politics. Now they were trying to purchase public opinion by buying newspapers, advertising, and issuing fake news. Such a course was futility itself, Irwin reported, undisturbed by the fact that journalistic support always seemed to be for sale. The solution was not without complication. Irwin regarded a dry America as unthinkable, for prohibition always resulted in bootlegging and further corruption. The answer seemed to be a combination of some vague sort of regulation and an internal clean-up by the beer and liquor interests themselves. But although the Prohibitionists achieved one success after another, the brewers refused to take heed. The facts of Irwin's study indicated that the nation was bound to move far along the road to enforced abstinence.[12]

Irwin also dealt with the problem of the "city boss." Bosses rose from the lower rungs of society—generally by saloon connections—with the aid of the usual combination of vice and big business, particularly the municipal service corporations. The resulting control was based on the power to grant special privilege. Had the machine never taken a dollar of the public money, Irwin pointed out, the health and growth of the city would still have been hurt by the discrimination that favoritism always meant.[13]

But the public was usually complacent. Either an "easy boss" such as Cox in Cincinnati ruled leniently, or the trial of the corruptor led to the gates of high finance and the rulers of the business world. Reform was always overwhelmed by respectability. "The crime of stealing means of production through corrupt legislatures and corrupt market manipulations," he wrote of the San Francisco graft prosecutions, "is as great and heinous, doubtless, as the crime of stealing silver spoons from the safe of a wealthy burgher; but enlightened public conscience has not risen yet to appreciate the equality in offense."[14]

A critical press, Irwin felt, was the answer to civic evils, and the struggle for control of the press ran through almost all of his articles. The beer and liquor interests sought to dominate it, and the bosses feared its power. The creation of a public conscience was in its hands. It was not surprising, therefore, that Irwin eventually turned to a study of the fourth estate.[15] The investigation had grown, Irwin stated in his autobiography, out of the repeated discovery by the muckrakers that "in cities where gangs of machine politicians were stealing the shingles off the city hall, often the local newspapers kept silent until some magazine writer like Lincoln Steffens came from outside to unsheath his rake."[16]

The newspapers, Irwin maintained, were essential to democracy since they supplied their readers with the new material of public opinion. This was particularly important in the twentieth century, he pointed out, because the constitution and laws, formed for an eighteenth-century civilization, were being warped awkwardly to fit the needs of a new industrial era. The press, as the strongest extra-judicial force outside of religion, had a vital public service role to play. This was not happening. To many proprietors, a paper was strictly a business proposition. They editorialized in their news columns and kept silent about corporate greed and special privilege. They bowed to the power of their advertisers and big business. They suppressed important news and dispensed private justice through the power to mention or ignore.

Initially Irwin had maintained that a business orientation was not a matter of moral turpitude. However, as the series progressed, he tended to change his point of view; honesty was no longer enough. He began to suggest vaguely that the close relation of the press with capital was a new kind of deeper dishonesty. This association created a censorship which had meant the preservation of boss rule in cities like Pittsburgh and Cincinnati.

The conservatism of the press was most clearly demonstrated by the Associated Press. The AP was not venal, he explained. Such criticism "only illustrates an American habit of mind. When we find any institution going wrong, we think first of individual dishonesty. We have not learned . . . to attribute the unfair working of social forces to faults in the system of things." The press had been corrupted by respectability and had become in the main a powerful force for reaction. On the other hand, William Randolph Hearst and the "yellow press," whatever they had done to taste, did espouse and crusade for the public interest.[17]

Despite the corruption of the cities, the corporations, and the press, Irwin did not believe that there were serious institutional inadequacies in American society. He suggested no legislative changes; the evils he had revealed seemed to be "the price we paid" for spectacular growth. The Standard Oil Company and the predatory railroads *did* produce service in the long run. The economic product was good, or the consumer would not have stood for it. The trouble seemed to lie only in distribution, which Irwin separated from the productive process. If the magnate became too careless, there was always the danger of competition and boycott.[18]

Thus in the long run the truth would out and virtue triumph. The best means to achieve this end was a free press. If the press seemed somewhat bound at the moment, the cure lay within journalism itself. Laws, here as elsewhere, would accomplish little. Eventually the newspapers would have to create their own integrity. Irwin had no doubt but that they would do so. A kept institution always lost its vitality and died; only an independent one was dynamic enough to live. Will Irwin had, as he maintained in his autobiography, a basic though somewhat inarticulate belief in the American competitive system. It seemed so obvious to him that it would work, that he never felt it necessary to reason out just why.

❧ 5 ❧

COMPETITION II:

BURTON JESSE HENDRICK

AND IDA M. TARBELL

Burton J. Hendrick and Ida M. Tarbell also believed in the workings of the competitive economic mechanism. They differed from Lewis and Irwin in that they undertook to explain the nature of the corporate activity which all of them saw as the central factor in the accumulation of wealth and the corruption of society.

The first of Hendrick's muckraking articles was written in praise of the newly enacted New York City tenement law, and how even this limited reform had taken a long struggle against corrupt politicians and vested interests such as the real estate associations, contractors, and Trinity Church.[1] When he joined *McClure's* in 1905, he went further into his investigation of municipal life. His favorite topic was the growing wealth of the Astor family, "the greatest absentee landlord in the world." Living upon unearned increment, such landlords made their greatest profits from the tenement dwellings which they rented to immigrants. Since men were to a large degree creatures of circumstances, their well-being was dictated by climate, food, occupation, social and economic conditions. The provision of a healthful and wholesome environment was essential.[2]

Hendrick soon progressed beyond attributing the ills of society solely to evil men and human greed. He found them instead in the institutionalization of the situation. In 1908 he wrote that the greatest problem of the day was corporate lawlessness. The corporations had captured the instrumentalities established for their regulation. Beneath the prosperity of America was an alliance between finance and politics. Corporation money financed political campaigns. State legislatures and regulatory bodies were corrupted, and the "exploitive spirit" was growing everywhere.[3]

Hendrick highlighted these evils in his two most comprehensive adventures in exposure: "The Story of Life Insurance" and "Great American Fortunes and Their Making." The first was an account of how the life insurance companies had shifted their main effort from providing insurance to engaging in financial enterprise.[4] By the twentieth century they had their subsidiary banks, extravagantly paid officials, strings of office buildings, alliances with Wall Street, and corruptionists in state capitals. Reform, however, could not be successful if it came solely from the outside. The policy holders had to assume responsibility for the actual operations of the industry.

In the "Great American Fortunes and Their Making," Hendrick described the 'trolleyization' of New York City through the exploitation of municipal utilities by the Widener-Whitney-Ryan syndicate.[5] They showed no interest in providing service. It was all a great brokerage operation. Profit came from watered stock, wasteful and dishonest construction, inadequate service, tax avoidance, and the failure to provide even elementary safety precautions. The syndicate had been able to get away with all this because it corrupted the legislature, the courts, and public opinion.

In the favorite form of the exposure literature, Hendrick devoted most of his attention to narrative history. The path of individual men along the road to success was minutely described. Only the strong succeeded where lesser men failed, and Hendrick's admiration for the financier was often ill-disguised. Although he had shown no liking for the tight-fisted Astors, he seemed indignant over the Vanderbilt progeny who were dissipating their inheritance. August Belmont made a killing, he reported, but was weak, and later capitulated, leaving control to stronger men. The "humiliation of the Goulds," he wrote, "is found in the character of the Goulds themselves. The complex forces controlling modern American industrialism have proved too much for them." Not so Charles Widener, W. C. Whitney, Thomas F. Ryan, or E. H. Harriman.[6] Fortunately for the public, other men of strength such as Charles Evans Hughes, Woodrow Wilson, and William G. McAdoo devoted their energies to the service of the public interest.[7]

The solution to the current evils of wealth and corporate power lay in an awakened, concerned populace. No theme was more frequent in Hendrick's writings. The impetus for reform, however, seemed again and again to come from above. Wilson, Hughes and William S. U'Ren were his special heroes because they won their struggles through moral force and the appeal to public opinion, rather than through copying methods of the bosses. The great success story for democracy was Oregon. By the use of initiative and referendum, the electorate had effected a quiet revolution. "Political power in Oregon," Hendrick wrote, "had been transferred from the bosses and the corporations to the citizenship."[8]

The reader, however, might have questioned the staying power of the public conscience. Within a few years, after Hendrick praised reform in New York State, he was lamenting that the bosses were back in control in Albany. If the danger had come from entrenched corruption and selfishness, how might honesty and service be institutionalized? This could be done if the people would use their legal right to control the corporations. According to the common law, he pointed out, the people had the power to supervise, regulate, and demand service of the corporations which they had chartered.[9] The competitive system was still practical and desirable, and it could be preserved by state and—to a much lesser degree—national regulation. Monopoly and bigness were clearly not in the public interest. Hendrick summed up his views on that subject when, in 1912, he wrote that "for several years college professors, Wall Street operators, leading railroad experts, and many of our foremost legislators have been saying that railroad monopoly was not only inevitable, but highly desirable. . . . The New Haven monopoly has benefited neither its own stockholders nor the public . . . and New England . . . pays higher prices and gets poorer service than under the old competitive system."[10]

The Interstate Commerce and Sherman Anti-trust acts could bring reform if they were not weakened or destroyed by capital or the unions. Assuming an equality of position between organized employers and employees, Hendrick talked of the unionism of 1894 as "well entrenched" and "successful." Using the Pullman strike as an example of the labor menace, he belabored Eugene V. Debs and the American Railway Union for tying up transportation in order to push their "private grievances with their employer."[11] It seemed to Hendrick that what he was to characterize as the "decently behaving, self-respecting, intelligent working class which is so generally believed to be the fundamental hope and safeguard of America"[12] had to be protected against itself.

Hendrick feared the aggregation of corporate wealth far more than the danger of labor combination. Corporation control of government was always a possibility as long as the political bosses existed. It was at the state level that the problem had to be solved, for Hendrick was extremely wary of placing enlarged powers in the hands of the national administration. The Federal government was not as venal as the state governments, but the threat was there. If it were permitted to increase its functions and powers, any subsequent corruption would be devastating. Hendrick did not consider the possibility of a reform role being played in the nation's capital.[13]

In writing of the experience of Oregon with the initiative and referendum, Hendrick declared that "for the first time a large group of American citizens have become concretely articulate in their political ideals" and have provided "an insight into the American conscience." His fellow voters had revealed themselves as cautious and close-fisted where governmental spending was concerned. They favored political home rule and believed in the value of higher education. They were against corruption, vote-buying, and graft, but were not necessarily opposed to the corporations as such. The American voters, in short, were not in favor of newfangled ideas; they were naturally conservative.[14] Burton J. Hendrick's "articulate citizens" looked very much like himself.

Of the muckrakers who believed in the working of a competitive mechanism, only Ida Tarbell described what the United States would look like under such a system. To Will Irwin, Burton Hendrick, and Alfred Henry Lewis it was American enterprise with the dishonesty and the great fortunes wrung out—it was the natural working out of things. For Ida Tarbell it was the early days of the oil region. The picture she drew was one of exuberant individualism developing a vast natural wealth, and creating a forward-looking society. The value of the oil fields of western Pennsylvania, Ida Tarbell believed, had to be measured not only by the new economic product, but also by the life of the people who produced the new wealth. They were happy and earnest; in their own individualistic way they were meeting their problems and giving a meaning to their lives that was not to be found in the financial ledger. Each entrepreneur had a fierce pride in his work and independence.

His business was his life. When the growth of the oil monopoly forced him out of business it was not merely an economic reverse but a personal tragedy.[15]

The two underlying assumptions of *The History of the Standard Oil Company* were that the monopoly had destroyed healthy individualism, and that it had done so by methods that were tragically illegal and immoral. The first assumption seemed inevitably to imply the second. If competition were a vital and dynamic state, then it could not have been overwhelmed by open and legal means.

In order to show this, Ida Tarbell carefully rejected the arguments which favored the existence of Standard Oil. John D. Rockefeller had not acted in self-defense, for he had been making a profit and was in no danger. The brains and capital necessary for the industry's development would have been available without his intercession. Indeed, she maintained, the most important technological advances in the industry had been introduced as a result of independent competition, over the opposition of Standard Oil. Nor had Standard provided cheap oil. Monopoly meant that prices were kept artifically high. The Standard Oil Company, after having made generous allowances for depreciation, paid annual profits of fifty percent of its initial capitalization. The price of oil was deliberately kept high, and economies effected through size and efficiency were given to the public only under pressure. The statistics showed that consumers had always paid more than they would have paid under a competitive price system. This, Ida Tarbell explained, was the motive for combination.[16]

Quite clearly then, the oil trust must have risen through guile and chicanery rather than from any natural benefits accruing from size. It is not surprising, therefore, that *The History of the Standard Oil Company* was primarily a tale of illegal behavior. It was the story of the "big hand" which had reached out to steal the conquests of the men of the oil fields.[17]

In her autobiography, Ida Tarbell was to claim that she never opposed bigness *per se*,[18] but this was certainly not the message of her *History*. "Human experience," she wrote, "long ago taught us that if we allowed a man or a group of men autocratic power . . . they used that power to oppose or defraud the public."[19] Such was her case against Standard Oil.

Standard produced one-third and controlled all but ten percent of the supply of petroleum. It had the strength to undersell its rivals, cut off their supplies and make it impossible for them to do business. However, the key to the power of the trust lay in its influence over transportation. Standard's annual profit was too large a sum to be consumed. Most of it was invested in the railroads which were the transporters as well as the users of Standard's products. Every year the Standard Oil Company widened this investment, "wiping up the property most essential to preserving and broadening its power." Already Rockefeller men were directors of almost all of the great railroads, as well as sharing power in such enterprises as Amalgamated Copper, the Steel Trust, and the National City Bank of New York. In addition, Standard controlled potential freight in oil, timber, acids, iron and many other products. Furthermore, through its own wealth and influence in the market, it would manipulate the price of railroad stock or make it impossible for the carriers to obtain any investment funds at all.[20]

The story of the rise of the oil trust had been one of illegal favoritism granted it by the railroads. The smaller oil producers and refiners had not been able to compete against this advantage. If the others in the industry also sought rebates—a consideration on which Ida Tarbell did not dwell—then Standard Oil had organized the practice on a scale beyond precedent. Drawbacks, the practice of getting rebates on other people's shipments, were a unique Rockefeller creation. Rockefeller had used his power over the railroads in order to build up his monopoly in oil. This control was the key to dealing with the trusts. So long as Standard Oil controlled transportation it would remain master of the industry. Investigations, laws against underselling, and anti-trust legislation such as the Sherman Act were not important.[21]

The solution had to be both political and ethical. Public opinion was to be the motivating force. The electorate needed to exercise its sovereign rights and pass laws for Federal supervision of transportation. But regulation was not enough to turn a "bad" corporation into a "good" one. The end of discrimination in transportation would stop the unfair advantages which the oil trust enjoyed, and in time would mean its decline and eventual destruction.[22] In achieving the suppression of monopolies, articulate public opinion was to act as the determining force. Ida Tarbell's *History* was directed as much as anything else at stimulating popular distaste for trust methods. This was the ethical side of the struggle. The greatest cost of Standard Oil was to be measured in moral rather than economic terms. America was a commercial nation which gloried in economic productivity. Business achievement justified any means by which it was attained. To get ahead in any way possible had become the highest moral goal. According to this criterion John D. Rockefeller was "the most successful man in the world."[23]

Ida Tarbell felt that this new set of values which she strongly attacked had been in large part the contribution of John D. Rockefeller. In building his great organization, he had spread his own code of business morality among the people. It featured hypocrisy and cynicism through the use of force, bribery, and chicanery. Even his donations to education and religion had helped extend the harm by depriving those forces of their independence and giving an added cloak of respectability to his own activities. The gifts carried with them, she wrote, the Rockefeller message that might made right, which threatened to saturate American life with "commercial Machiavellism."[24]

The dream which lay behind *The History of the Standard Oil Company* was the restoration of competition. In such a world, an ethical and moral regeneration would take place. There would be an increasing scorn of unfair play and a disdainful ostracism of those who used unfair means or sought special privileges. The new creed would take away the automatic mantle of justification from weath and in its place leave the realization that "success won by unfair means is not worth winning."[25]

Although Ida Tarbell wrote about the fight against the street railway magnates in Chicago, lauded Governor Charles Evans Hughes of New York, and expressed an interest in tenement reform,[26] her principal efforts were focused on two subjects: the Standard Oil Company and the tariff. The latter series was not as successful as *The History of the Standard Oil Company,* for she had had no personal knowledge of the subject and wrote what she herself later described as a second-hand study.[27] In detailing the history of tariff legislation in the United States, she was primarily interested in showing that high rates were the result of a coalition between the manufacturers and the politicians. As in the case of Standard Oil, the most important measurement of the tariff was in the individuals it made. The results in both cases were the same: men deficient in self-respect, indifferent to the dignity of Congress, willing to bribe, barter, and juggle the truth. Ethical considerations had been cast out from the world of business, and with their departure had come shoddy goods, the destruction of the instinct of workmanship, and a weakening of the spirit of self-reliance. The tariff was, she feared, destroying the spiritual basis of democracy.[28]

In both of her major works Ida Tarbell evidenced a somewhat limited conception as to what constituted problems of business ethics. Low wages, bad working and living conditions, the exploitation of woman and child labor, poverty, and high prices were evils that ought to be changed. They were not, however, basic problems of morality. That issue, in her view, was concerned with business privilege, poor workmanship, corruption, and the destruction of intellectual and business independence and individual initiative. To the muckrakers further to the left, the economic exploitation of underprivileged groups and classes was essentially a moral problem. It led them to seek substantial and often drastic changes in the organization of society. In separating exploitation and ethics, Ida Tarbell was implicitly limiting the amount and degree of reform that was necessary. The assumption seemed to be that the evils of an inequalitarian society would be corrected by a competitive business world which would restore self-reliance and commercial honesty.

All of the muckraker proponents of competition believed that in the final analysis everything depended on public opinion. In this reliance they did not depart substantially from the views of the other journalists of exposure. Where they did differ was in their conception of the use to which popular sentiment should be put. While the more radical journalists sought to focus it as a force for definite legislative ends and unselfish service devoted to the communal good, the believers in competition had a different understanding. Public opinion was but the total of all of the individual beliefs. Alfred Henry Lewis, Will Irwin, Burton Hendrick, and Ida Tarbell asked only that the people uphold the laws by giving up their subservience to wealth. They believed that the system was sound and that, with various amounts of tinkering, it would continue to work well. Samuel Hopkins Adams and Thomas Lawson focused their attention on a more detailed study of the particular economic mechanisms of Wall Street and the stock market. They believed that drastic action was needed in order to make the financial machinery of the nation operate for the public good.

❧ 6 ❧

REGULATION OF WALL STREET:

SAMUEL HOPKINS ADAMS

AND THOMAS W. LAWSON

One of the traditional themes of American democracy has been protest against the growth of a centralized money power in private hands. The early followers of Thomas Jefferson opposed the First Bank of the United States, and those of Andrew Jackson helped bring about the liquidation of the Second. In the early years after the Civil War, speculators such as Daniel Drew, Jim Fisk, and Jay Gould were able to make large fortunes by wrecking corporations through over-capitalization and manipulation. Particularly in the agrarian states of the West and South was there mounting criticism of the control of money and credit on "the street." In the 1890's the investment bankers used their power over the sources of capital to take control of much of the nation's business and industry. The United States passed into the period of finance capitalism. Although this had been undertaken partially to rationalize and stabilize the organization of industry, there were enormous profits to be made. Under the two-fold burden of speculation and capitalization, the stock market and the business community staggered uncertainly onward during the muckrake era. Financial upsets in 1903 and 1907, the New York insurance and Stock Exchange investigations, and finally a Congressional investigation by the Pujo Committee, all pointed to market irregularities and financial concentration.

The journalists of exposure presented the facts which fueled the fires of protest that led to investigation and later reform. However, many of the muckrakers were not at home when dealing with economic problems, and their solutions often lacked the authority of their exposés. Corporate power "ought to be controlled," they felt, but they rarely said how. Samuel Hopkins Adams and Thomas W. Lawson undertook the task of suggesting specific financial reforms. Adams, who had made his reputation uncovering the patent medicine frauds, feared economic concentration but rarely suggested sweeping reform. However, stirred by a symposium on high prices and the rising cost of living, he wrote a trenchant attack on the financial interests and offered his ideas for a solution. Tom Lawson, having run with the wolves of Wall Street as one of the most notorious traders on the curb, turned to the side of the sheep to expose the practices of his erstwhile companions. He led an eager magazine-reading public through the sensational though tangled path of *Frenzied Finance*. A number of years later when his banner had become sullied and his following dissipated, he returned to the struggle to explain the real meaning of his story and to suggest a substantial remedy. Both Lawson and Adams highlighted to the American people the nature and problems of financial organization.

Samuel Hopkins Adams was not the first to write about the patent medicine racket. A government chemist, Doctor Harvey Wiley, had been battling against the poisonous drugs that paraded as the poor man's doctor. Edward Bok's *Ladies' Home Journal* had already attacked the harmful nostrums, and *Collier's* editor Norman Hapgood was conducting a campaign against them. Hapgood became involved in a controversy with

William Jennings Bryan over the truth of the patent medicine advertisements, and picked Adams, who had written a number of articles on public health, to investigate the industry.

Adams was followed by detectives and threatened with lawsuits and personal violence, but he "gloried in the combat." In a running series of more than twenty articles, Samuel Hopkins Adams told the story of the medicinal frauds.[1] The manufacturers, he contended, mispresented their products which they filled full of alcohol and habit-forming drugs. They "buncoed the public out of millions, in the vending of the Pierce Remedies, Swamp Root, Duffy's Malt Whisky, Lydia Pinkham's preparation, and all of that class."[2] The most significant picture that emerged from Adam's writing was the economic and political power of the purveyors of "poison for profit." It was no wonder that one of the "barons" of the industry had told Adams all of the facts about his "cure" which seemed too safely "protected" to be attacked. News derogatory to the patent medicines was never printed because of muzzling clauses in advertising contracts. The purpose of advertising was not only to sell the product but to exert pressure on the press. The drug magnates were not alone in that endeavor, Adams pointed out. Others such as the railroads and theatres also bullied the press, but he felt that the poison purveyors were the worst offenders. The press in turn pressured the politicians to prevent any regulatory legislation which might curtail a lucrative source of income. Of about $100 million taken in yearly by the medicinal trust, approximately forty percent was applied to building up this extremely potent pressure group. Such tactics were possible because of the money-making orientation of journalism. The publishers were businessmen. The newspaper chains were particularly acquiescent and even some religious papers offered their editorial columns to the quacks. "Religious!" Adams exploded, "Their tongue is set on fire of hell."[3]

His initial optimism about the effects of publicity and the

labeling of drug ingredients soon faded. Despite the effectiveness of publicity in cutting down the profits of the patent medicine manufacturers, the Administration and the courts carved the heart out of any regulatory laws. Judicial blindness and governmental favoritism formed a dangerous kind of conservatism which became one of Adam's basic themes. *"It is the law that is being poisoned,"* he wrote in 1910, *"and in its corruption every citizen is corrupted.* To bind the law itself in the coils of a legal procedure, to subvert the people's expressed will . . . is anarchism more subtle than the cult of the most destructive philosophy, more deadly than the threat of dynamite and of the crimson flag."[4]

As editorial chief for the short-lived *Ridgway's* magazine, Adams crystalized his attitude toward the growing power of the business interests. The trust had become the leading national institution and he was opposed to it. Its mere existence was a menace to the law. If the trusts were not checked, he warned, they might in time seek to take over the government. The "needs" of giant business combinations led them sooner or later into politics. They destroyed competition and sought special privileges. They secured higher tariffs, paid low wages, utilized child labor, neglected elementary safety precautions, and complained of paternalism, anarchism, and class hatred every time they were subjected to criticism. Their power over the press and the courts became Adams' most frequent topic and greatest alarm.[5]

Even so, Samuel Hopkins Adams was fundamentally optimistic and believed in the strength of America and its ideals. This faith was something that he rarely questioned and which he therefore did not feel impelled to describe or explain. No matter how widespread and pernicious the graft, it could not be expected to continue. In the long run, problems were slowly being met and solved. He wrote about what was wrong in order that it might be corrected; that it would eventually be corrected, he did not doubt. The actual reforms that Adams suggested prior to his principal exposition in 1910 were relatively minor. They were directed at specific abuses and did not touch the larger problems which he pointed out. These were apparently left to a slowly progressing and basically sound America. His answer to the evils of the patent medicines was labeling, publicity, and the Pure Food and Drug Act. For the power of railroad corruption, it was the Elkins Act, though he would have liked to see the rebater jailed. He supported the Beveridge Law to protect child labor. Although strongly opposed to special privilege, he tended to place his ultimate reliance on public opinion to restrict it. Apathy and the popular belief that the United States was a "business nation" had blunted the general sense of public welfare. Adams' investigations of patent medicines, slum conditions, disease and epidemics clarified for him the role of the private interests that lay behind the "public murders" by the unchecked plague and the bottled poison. His experience, he wrote, had deprived him of that "knock-kneed reverence for Business Interests which is the glorious heritage of every true American." These interests, were "always a malign influence, and usually an incredibly stupid one."[6]

In 1910, commenting on a symposium in *Cosmopolitan* on the high cost of living, Adams presented his only systematic program of reform. The two problems were the trusts and over-capitalization, whose operation he vividly described. His solution to the centralization of wealth was a counter-centralization of power. This meant supervision and control of the trusts by a governmental body which had the authority to say "You shall not charge one fraction of a mill above what will give you a fair return on a fairly estimated investment." This would be made practical by commissions which would set the limits of railroad and industrial capitalization.

Such a program, Adams warned, would immediately lead to

the rise of the old cries of "Socialism." This, as he had commented earlier in *Ridgway's,* was the "old game of trying to befool the people by a catchword." What mattered was that the steps he had outlined were necessary, whatever they were called. The only alternative to rigid, detailed, centralized control was starvation. Immediate action was necessary "lest . . . the consumer become the consumed."[7]

Thomas W. Lawson's *Frenzied Finance*[8] was the true confession of his liaison with the outstanding trust of the day. However, he maintained, his exposés were not the vengeful revelations of a rejected lover but rather an attempt to bring his former favorite over to the side of morality. Wall Street controlled the United States and the Standard Oil Company was at its center. With its mines in the West, factories in the East, colleges in the South, and churches in the North, it was the climax of the power of dollars. Where Ida Tarbell had been concerned with the way in which John D. Rockefeller had gathered together so large a part of the productive capacity of the nation, Thomas Lawson chronicled the growth of Standard Oil's empire of money under the leadership of Henry H. Rogers. The financial interests had reached their highest point of influence in the history of the United States. They controlled laws and legislatures and ran politics, molded public opinion and determined the verdicts of the courts themselves.

What really bothered Lawson, though, was more mathematical in nature. The power of the "System" came from its hold on the money supply of the nation. The life and fire insurance companies, banks, corporations, and the stock exchanges had been corrupted and diverted from their proper function. By bribery and juggling the Standard Oil men took control of the small investor's money and used it to rig the market for more.

In his articles, Lawson chaotically narrated the story of his connection with the gas company wars in Boston and the building of the copper trust. He reconstructed incidents with full dialogue, naming names of the prominent men of business and finance as wrong-doers, and recounting a series of midnight maneuvers, flights to avoid prosecution, and sickbed denunciations. The reading public was fascinated and the circulation of *Everybody's* quadrupled to almost a million monthly copies in 1905.

The biggest reaction resulted from revelations that were merely incidental to Lawson's story. He had mentioned the manner in which insurance company funds were used by the "System," and the questions and subscriptions poured in. Responding to his audience, Lawson announced "I am going to cause a life-insurance blaze." The assets of the three great companies, New York Life, Equitable, and Mutual Life, were controlled by the J. P. Morgan and Standard Oil interests; the policy holders had no say in their disposition. At the same time that the insiders raked in millions through stock speculation, premium rates went up and dividends declined. The reserves were being dissipated so quickly that a crash seemed inevitable. Lawson called for a thorough investigation followed by regulation of investment to prevent all connections between the insurance companies and the big banking houses.[9]

On this subject, Lawson made an important contribution to public awakening. His efforts were instrumental in bringing about the Armstrong Committee investigation—through which Charles Evans Hughes achieved fame as counsel—and a partial reform of the methods of the industry. Usually, however, Lawson saw no further than the stock exchanges and the financial manipulations of the "System." He himself had only been concerned with the financial side of business, never with actual production of goods. Between the two he drew a definite line.

Lawson's conception of legitimate enterprise was his grand plan for an empire in copper. All the mining property was to be brought together into one unit and stocks and bonds issued up to its full potential value. He showed no interest in increased productivity, greater efficiency, or lower prices. The industry had attracted him in the first place because it had been so profitable. The only "public-spirited" aspect of his plan was that the small investors would be allowed to subscribe to his undertakings. They could get part of the profits which would be guaranteed by the maintenance of a stable market. This itself was to be achieved by keeping the vast bulk of the stock for the insiders who would benefit immensely as values went up. If they owned a large enough block, be believed, they would not find it worth while to manipulate the market to swallow up the small investment of the general public. His plan, however, failed. Not only were the outsiders looted by the directors of the "System," but so too was Thomas Lawson. This had caused the breach with his fellow jugglers of Standard Oil.

Lawson claimed that his muckrake intentions were more than revenge or mere exposure; *Frenzied Finance* was to prepare the way for reform. He himself had The Remedy which he would keep secret until "the people" were set for it. Its main element seemed to involve the outlay of vast sums of money which he claimed a syndicate of French bankers had offered to supply, and which, amazingly, Lawson apparently had not accepted.[10] What Lawson had in mind was a vast manipulation of the market itself, and there was a certain degree of superficial logic to his idea. If the "System" fed upon the money supplied by the innocent public, small investors might end this by getting out of the game by selling all of their stocks and bonds. In the years 1905 and 1906, Lawson appeared to be engaged in an enormous "bear" raid on the Street, while he also sought enough proxies to take control of the insurance industry.[11] However, even if the purity of his motives were assumed, the deeper logic of these activities would seem questionable. If the "interests" inflicted hardship upon the public by juggling values, was counter-manipulation the correct remedy?

Most of the serious criticism of Lawson was not concerned with the accuracy of his story but with the honesty of his motives. His career on Wall Street had amounted to a vast "bucket shop" wherein he drew his strength primarily from his ability to affect the market. Through the development of the advertising and publicity media, he gave continual advice and information to a large number of small investors. Because of his ability to reach this highly unorganized and volatile source of funds, Lawson had been taken on as a temporary partner of the Standard Oil group which was floating a copper trust.

The direction of most of his big market enterprises had been definitely in a bearish direction. He seemed to find it easier to gain profits by tearing down rather than by building up the value of stocks. Such had been his venture in the Lamson Cash Carrier Company, and when he was hired to build up the competitive position of Westinghouse on the Stock Exchange. he did it by almost destroying General Electric. Conversely. Lawson suffered his own worst financial defeats when he tried to create a rising market in copper. He was, at least by experience, a wrecker,[12] and despite his protestations, Lawson was clearly out for revenge. When he struck back at his former allies "in copper" it had resulted in the fairly considerable Wall Street disturbance of December 1904.

In considering the muckrakers as constructive reformers, Lawson's motivation is an important factor. He alone among the journalists of exposure was seriously embarrassed by such a question. During the time that he was writing *Frenzied Finance,* he continued to use his following to manipulate stocks for his own benefit. In response to criticism, he sputtered that his predictions were wrong because the "interests" were doing everything they could to discredit him, even to the extent of juggling prices to disprove his forecasts. Everything he did on the Street was only to defeat the "System."[13]

Everybody's editor, E. J. Ridgway, sorrowfully wrote him a public letter saying, "I shall never cease to believe that if you had kept out of Wall Street after you began the series with us, you would be the biggest man in the country to-day."[14] The more sympathetic critics believed that Lawson's motives were a mixture of sincerity and a desire for personal gain, and all agreed that he had badly weakened his case.[15] Frank Fayant, in *Success,* perceptively listed four motives for his activities. They were revenge, fame, reform, and money.[16] A further factor which should be considered was Lawson's excitement over the Wall Street "game." In a fictionalized biography, David Graham Phillips, acutely offered an explanation. Phillips' Mathew Blacklock justified buying a particular stock, while advising his followers to sell, with the explanation that "All I shall say is that it was business, that in such extreme and dire compulsion as was mine, it was—and is—right under the code, the private and real Wall Street code."[17]

There may well have been a division between Lawson's simultaneous roles of crusader and financier, but the most convincing explanation is that there was a confusion of all of the various aspects. Lawson himself had a ferocious belief in his own composite integrity. No matter of whom he wrote, from the Puritan fathers to an epigrammatic composite of the "Good Man," it was always a self-portrait. His conception of reform was largely that of a great crusade with the details somewhat blurred, of which Thomas Lawson was the leader.[18]

The first phase was exposure of the "System" during which he expected to create a vast and loyal following among the American people. Then he would lead them to the promised land. It seemed to him to be sufficient to inform his followers that he would be their guide; he felt no compulsion to provide details as to the route to be followed or the goal to be sought.

The failure of the people to yield unqualifiedly to Lawson's call was a matter of extreme anguish to him.[19] In continuing to play the market, they were only doing on a small scale what he was doing on a larger one. Perhaps this was why they failed to follow him. It was all very well for rich men to lure investors into gambling on stocks in order to make them wealthy, but Lawson had promised to make them pure. Although the public was willing to follow his advice on securities, it did not seek him out as a leader. This was the flaw in his great crusade.

The conservative *Nation* explained, "Our sole point is that we must differentiate the evil and untrustworthy man as informer, as betrayer, as clamorer, from the evil and untrustworthy man as reformer. In the former capacity he may enlighten the public; in the latter, it is preposterous to suppose that he can lead it." The moralistically-minded *Outlook* echoed, "It seems hardly credible that any man of intelligence can suppose that Mr. Lawson is engaged in an unselfish, moral, and public-spirited attempt to destroy the evils of speculating." Norman Hapgood in *Collier's* felt that he had "set in motion a force which will hardly stop short of serious reforms" but believed that Lawson's own movement might well break against the pillars of the good sense of the community.[20]

For several years Lawson continued to play coy about his remedy in the hope of building up a national following. Warning of the dangers of a premature disclosure, he wrote "as soon as it is before the people, all the energies of the "System," supported by untold millions, will be bent to prevent its adoption." Although his comings and goings were still considered newsworthy, much of his prestige among reformers and on the general market was gone. When in the fall of 1907 he revealed something of his "Remedy" in an open letter to Theodore Roosevelt, it stirred little interest.[21]

Within a few weeks he announced his retirement from muckraking. In typical Lawsonian prose he wrote to Ridgway: "You talk of what I owe the people. What do I owe to the gelatine-spined shrimps? What have the saffron-blooded apes done for me or mine that I should halt any decisions to match their lightning-change ten above-ten-below-zero chameleon-hued loyalty. The people! ... Forgive me, my dear Ridgway, but the people, particularly the American people, are a joke—a System joke."[22]

But although Lawson could not remain in the headlines, he could not keep out of the newspapers, and after a four-year period he attempted a comeback in the popular magazine.[23] The cover of *Everybody's* for October, 1912, promised "Here in this issue Thomas W. Lawson cuts loose 'THE REMEDY.' A Smash at the System's Solar-plexus." His analysis had developed considerably. The evil no longer was solely financial manipulation and the use of "the people's" savings. The issue had become the capital tax that was being levied on all the people through higher prices. Over the preceding forty years the national wealth had grown from twenty-five to one hundred and thirty-one billion dollars. Although all of the citizens produced it, a major part was owned by a few thousand. Of this amount, Lawson claimed, sixty billion was represented by stocks and bonds, two-thirds of which represented fictitious claims.[24]

His plan, he wrote, "aims to secure to every man his share in the national prosperity in proportion to his contribution." The factors which went into production were the labor of mind, body, machine, and capital. The last was simply the accumulation of the other three. Price, he felt, should ideally be determined in such a way that each of these kinds of effort received the full share of its contribution. Consumption would then equal production. If production were to rise beyond consumption, prices would fall and bring the two back into harmony. In twentieth-century America, however, as the material output advanced, so did its cost to the public. Obviously, Lawson felt, this was proof that an improperly large return was going to one of the components. The billions of dollars of over-capitalization, represented by watered stocks and bonds in the hands of a few, showed that it was capital that was taking the dishonestly big share.[25]

This unjust distribution of wealth was created through the stock exchange. Lawson's remedy, therefore, had two parts. First, control the machinery of the stock market and end its role as a gambling device and an unfair pricer. Then capitalization could be reduced to the actual investment involved. The inflation of stocks and bonds, speculation, sales on margin when delivery was not intended, unfairly large dividends, interest and undivided profits, interlocking directorates and contributions to political parties had to be forbidden. This was to be done by the Federal incorporation of exchanges. Those who violated the regulations would be forbidden the use of the mails.

Lawson was extremely vague about the second phase of his program. At first he had written about wringing dry the watered stock and making a "fair" division of what he said were the five billions of real money deposited in savings banks. However, once he finished setting forth the initial step, he never mentioned the second. Presumably it might have been similar to the one which he had described in his open letter to Theodore Roosevelt during the credit panic of 1907. Then he had suggested a Presidential board to appraise the value of securities, the condition of the banks, and the public-spiritedness of corporation directors. Whatever his ideas were in 1913, he did not say. By the time Lawson wrote of his Plan, the Pujo Committee was already systematically covering much the same field. The final articles of his series were devoted to a discussion of the testimony given before that body. He seemed not to feel that he and the Committee were in competition but rather that the investigation was engaged in further substantiating his own revelations. His view was not completely without justification, for his exposure had helped to stimulate public demand for information and correction.

His "Remedy" did create a certain amount of stir. Lawson's regulatory bill was introduced into the U. S. Senate by Senator Henry Ashurst of New Mexico, and Governor Hughes of New York did consult Lawson, as President Roosevelt had done at an earlier time.[26] Lawson always started out strong and with great fanfare, but he could not remain with one topic until he completed it. Sensational though his campaigns were, they never lived up to their promise. Although the would-be champion of the people attracted great public interest, he could not hold it. Thomas W. Lawson, the reformer, bore too great a resemblance to Thomas W. Lawson, the financier.

Samuel Hopkins Adams and Thomas Lawson focused their attention on Wall Street, which they believed was the central factor in the corruption of the national economic system. Their attack on the misdeeds of "high finance" was but a part of the spirit of reform that was growing in the land. Working on a larger canvas, Ray Stannard Baker represented the fervor and the breadth of the new demand for social reconstuction.

❦ 7 ❦

THE SEARCH FOR REFORM:

RAY STANNARD BAKER

At the beginning of the twentieth century, Ray Stannard Baker painted a picture of national progress and strength. Writing for *McClure's,* he dismissed Coxey's army and the silver agitators of 1896 as merely the usual protest of the debtor, but not typical of the country as a whole. What the individual ought to do was raise and better himself through initiative and self-control. When he wrote of industry, whether in the United States or Germany, Baker saw only its organized efficiency.[1]

Within a few years he changed his tune. He found industrial warfare and lawlessness, starving miners, anti-scab violence, labor bosses, and conspiracy between the unions and the trusts. The two giants squeezed the public which was powerless to do other than pay the bill for corruption and monopoly. What Baker feared was too great an aggregation of power on either side. The cure was up to the individual citizen.[2] Bossism in labor as in all other fields was a symptom of civic laziness: "If *you* want to be rid of the Boss in *your* city, *you* have to go to the primaries and election booth and protest and vote and protest again. If *you,* as a working-man, want honest and efficient unionism, *you* have got to go to the union meetings and make things right, and if *you* as a stockholder, want to see common business honesty in *your* trusts and in *your* corporations, you have got to look after the thing yourself." No matter what the evil was, Baker came back to the same solution: "if this republic is saved it must be saved by *individual effort.*"[3]

The response to these articles was extremely favorable, and Theodore Roosevelt called his account of lawlessness in Colorado "absolutely correct and fair." Of another of the articles, the President reported that he was most impressed by the lesson of personal responsibility which had been presented. "How emphatically this revelation emphasizes the need of drawing the line on conduct, among politicians, and among private individuals alike," he wrote. With a strong sense of service characteristic of the muckrakers, Baker wrote to his father that "it seems almost as though I had a mission to perform." The various exposés in *McClure's* were, he wrote shortly afterward, "doing more for stirring up the American people than any other publication ever did before." "I think we have struck the right Grail," he added.[4]

As he continued to write, he came to find that behind the excesses of labor were always those of capital and that the greatest renunciation of individual responsibility was in the corporation. Why did such unhealthy activities persist? In his notebooks, where he tested his ideas, Baker attempted a diagnosis. The disease was due to legislative lag. Despite enormous industrial development the country still operated under laws passed fifty to seventy-five years before for a competitive economy. Such a world, he had come to believe, was no longer operative. Talking about law enforcement was like saying "be good" to a railroad engineer whose engine was about to blow up. "The real remedy is," he continued, "... *economic facts* and the dose is to be applied to the people." Again and again in his notebooks Baker swore fealty to this task. "My job is illumination," he wrote, chanting, "educate, educate, educate."[5]

In 1905 Baker began to "educate" the public as to the nature of the railroad power in the United States. Its grants of favoritism were, he felt, the chief cause of the trusts. The barons of Wall Street unfairly taxed the consumers and stretched out from their vast transportation systems to take over other industries. By the time he finished his series, Baker had come to believe that unless a really good regulatory bill was passed, public pressure for government ownership might become irresistible. He replied to cries against such "confiscatory" action by asking if it was right for the railroads to take the people's property by unfair levies.[6]

Baker's study drew the applause from railroad experts, and President Roosevelt wrote: "I haven't a criticism to suggest. . . . You have given me two or three thoughts for my own message. It seems to me that one of the lessons you teach is that these railroad men are not to be treated as exceptional villains but merely ordinary Americans who under given conditions are by the mere force of events forced into doing much of which we complain." In return he sent the galleys of the message which he was preparing for Congress, but failed to accept Baker's suggestions for controlled minimum rates to prevent rebates.[7]

Yet Baker himself had already progressed beyond the belief that this would cure the railroad problem. In February, 1906, he visited the President and discussed the Hepburn bill. "Suddenly he asked me," Baker recorded, " 'If this is only a first step where do you think we are going?' 'You may not agree with me, Mr. President,' I said, 'but I believe we cannot stop short of governmental ownership of the railroads.' "[8] For the next three years Baker pondered over what should be done, moving reluctantly all the time toward socialism. This was clearest in the evolution of his conception of "individualism." The Socialists now seemed its best practitioners for they demanded duty and responsibility from each citizen. "Socialism may be wrong," he reflected, "in its ultimate program . . . but somehow I feel that I am going by the same road, that I am hoping the same hopes." Must we not have more socialism to get more individualism, he asked? Through his reading Baker had become convinced that man was not a victim of the merciless law of natural selection but was able to control such forces through his power to modify the workings of nature. This belief combined with the growth of monopoly had weaned him away from his initial belief in reform through the mechanism of increased competition.[9]

During 1906 Baker continually reflected on the merits and faults of socialism. One problem was that it placed undue emphasis on the material environment and the abolition of private property. Once we reach that point, he maintained, socialism will not be necessary because man will have been completely made over. However, socialism was an unselfish enthusiastic force and presented a positive program, much of which was good.[10]

By the spring of 1907 Baker felt even more closely committed to socialism. Two kinds of men were inclined toward it, he opined, the dreamer and those who "are backing toward socialism, repelled by the excesses of individualism. They see in socialism a handy weapon . . . and when the abuses from which they shrink are cured, they will part company straightway with the extremists. Of this latter class I consider myself a member. . . . And yet I admire the high & unselfish ideals of many socialists."[11]

In the spring of 1908, Baker's doctrinal yearnings were coming to a head. He was depressed by racial antagonism and disappointed by Roosevelt's economic conservatism. He felt that this was the most trying period of his life. Two libel suits, arising out of his railroad articles, went against him because of legal technicalities. "How can justice be expected," he asked in anguish, "when so many of our judges are defenders of railroad corporations & trusts? They hold back every sort of economic & social reform by strict interpretations of ancient law."[12] In his home in East Lansing, Michigan, his efforts to improve the school system and the State civil service had been unsuccessful. What weighed most heavily, however, was his strong feeling of the social failure of organized religion. He had been concerned with the building of a new church, and that led him to brood continually about the shortcomings of religion. The factor of brotherhood was left out. "The Socialists have a community spirit of service," Baker wrote. They offered "brotherhood nearer than anything I know to the *real church.*"

"From this time on," he asserted, "I am going to pursue this subject: *I must join something.* I shall look deeply into the subject of Socialism—I mean upon its organization side." With this, he began to work even harder to dispel the doubts that remained. "Intellectual individuality & freedom must not be confused with economic individualism," he wrote. "Intellectual individualism is quite compatible with economic Socialism." The Socialists were the only ones whose activities were basically religious.[13]

But Baker's hope was doomed to failure, for no one had the spiritual panacea he sought. Others operated on a material level: "If it were not for the Socialists, I should be a Socialist. Sitting at home, reading and thinking, dreaming of the ideal human state, I see that Socialism is, ultimately, the only way out. But when I attend Socialist meetings and hear the intemperate clamor of half ignorant men (themselves not prepared to exercise the self-restraint so necessary to Socialism, themselves not willing to become servants) I am afraid! How necessary is education, *education!* How great must be the patience of all leaders and idealists, that they do not lead too fast."

His disillusionment marked the passing of a definite stage. Although he continued to think about the Party, he did so with growing distaste. As he summed it up, "Socialism is *not religious* but economic. The great body of Socialists are not looking for ... opportunity to *serve society;* but for a better *distribution of wealth* ... they have not got beyond property-worship!" With a final renunciation, "No, Socialism does not go far enough for me. I demand not only a better system: but a higher individual character," Baker ceased the flirtation.[14]

Even so, his deliberations had done much to crystalize a collectivist concept of social action and his class analysis of historical movement. This was clear in his answer to the criticism which Theodore Roosevelt had made of his articles on the Negro. Class was the dynamic factor of change and Baker ascribed the President's political success to the leadership of just such an upheaval. "You underestimate the necessity and usefulness (in our present stage) of class action and class feeling, although, in your books you defend and approve of party action, which, if it has any vitality, is always, more or less, a class action. If this were not the time of loosened party lines and of readjustment ... in which personality for the moment rises superior to platform, such a leader as you are, Mr. President, would be an impossibility."[15]

In his articles, Baker cautiously steered away from any espousal of socialism, using it rather as a bogey to advance more moderate steps.[16] Nevertheless, the development of his social philosophy was mirrored in a series of articles on the Negro. Although infinitely complicated by racial animosity, the problem of the Negro was part and parcel of the big issue which beset the age. Slavery had been abolished, he maintained, because it was undemocratic. The ferment of the Negro, then, was but one part of a world-wide struggle. "The underman will not keep his place," Baker explained. "Thus we see the growth of labour organizations, the spread of populists and socialists, who demand new rights and a greater share in the products of labour."[17]

It was natural that Baker also considered racial conflict as a spiritual problem. His search for individual and national reform was a moral quest more than anything else, and he himself sought a spiritual movement to which he might belong. His David Grayson stories of rural contentment were in part a response to this need, as was his flirtation with the Socialist Party.[18] He became disillusioned with the latter because it lacked real unselfishness and community spirit. "How I am driven back again & again upon Jesus Christ," he reflected during the trying spring of 1908. "The more I think of human ills and social remedies, the more I see that the teachings of Jesus Christ is the only solution. Far, far beyond socialism (which is a mechanism of social force: not spiritual) stands the unreached Christ in love & serenity."[19]

The result was a series of articles on the failure of the churches.[20] Describing them as "a mere human agency for fostering religion," Baker felt that the Protestant churches had lost their spiritual leadership and no longer had any message for common people. There was a growing class division within the temples of God, but the greatest separation seemed to be that those with money were inside and the poor were outside. The Church needed to do two things: inspire the individual with a belief in divine power, and draw all men together in a democratic relationship. There was a highly religious quality in dedicating oneself to the abolition of poverty. The best chance of such a movement within organized religion came from the 'New Christianity' of Walter Rauschenbusch and the leaders of the social gospel philosophy. In an address at Amherst College Baker summed up the message of faith that ran through *The Spiritual Unrest*. The great American accomplishment had been production, but it had come at great cost to children, families, immigrants, workers and the Negro. The real test of national strength was to be found in how the weak were treated. The ideal of service was Christian as well as democratic.[21]

The groundwork of Baker's muckraking articles had been the various social ferments at work in national life. Impending change was his clearest theme. It continually appeared in his titles as well as in the text, and he continually sought a role which he himself could play. Realizing that sooner or later in a democracy everything was carried into the political arena, he became increasingly interested in politics. At the same time his attitude toward Theodore Roosevelt was changing. For many years T.R. had symbolized political action to Baker. He warmly admired Roosevelt and sought to win him to a deeper understanding of the 'true' forces of the times. Although Baker's exasperation grew, he had always praised T.R. publicly. However, as the Progressive movement gathered political steam in 1910, Baker finally gave up hope. After two visits to Oyster Bay during which he attempted to persuade the ex-president to take a 'more enlightened' view on national issues, particularly the tariff, Baker at last despaired. T.R. had served his purpose, he recorded in his notebook, but the old type of politics was gone and the Rough-rider had to go with it.[22]

The "aggression of capitalism" had reached the oppressive stage and the public was willing to struggle against it. The old party lines had become meaningless, Baker believed, as everything polarized around the big issue. In the fields in which competition had been replaced by monopoly, the government must either regulate or take possession. Baker's own sympathies were all in the latter direction. The key to a new realignment appeared to be the insurgent forces led by Senator Robert M. La Follette of Wisconsin. Here was an upheaval drawing its primary strength from the West which Baker so loved, yet reaching throughout the nation. At last Baker seemed to have found a cause and an organization of which he could be part, which appeared to offer the necessary spiritual values. In his articles of 1910 he summed up the progress of the insurgents as "a new moral force ... abroad in the land."[23]

During 1910 and 1911 Baker founded a local Insurgents' Club, edited La Follette's autobiography, and became one of the circle of advisers that gathered about the insurgent leader. In an article explaining "The Meaning of Insurgency," Baker wrote that the Greenbackers and Populists had kept the desire for democracy alive in the nation. Now the journalists of exposure were educating the public to the concrete nature of the menace of concentrated wealth and monopoly. "They were unpalatable facts which the muck-rakers presented," he wrote, "but they were facts; proof was piled upon proof, certainty was added to certainty, so that even the prosperous and naturally conservative jury of the whole people were thoroughly convinced. And now we are in the midst of a . . . great wave of political insurgency; and this wave, please God, is going over the ramparts; something will be done." The insurgent movement and a peaceful national revolution seemed the logical outcome of the era of the muckrakers.[24]

Ray Stannard Baker demonstrated that the drive for national reform could favor a high degree of government intervention in the economy without espousing a rigid doctrinaire philosophy. He had tested the merits of the Socialist Party and found them wanting. Lincoln Steffens and David Graham Phillips reluctantly discovered that their quest for social progress led them much closer to socialism.

❧ 8 ❧

TRAVELERS ALONG THE WAY:

LINCOLN STEFFENS

AND DAVID GRAHAM PHILLIPS

Lincoln Steffens and David Graham Phillips went far along the path to socialism. They did not join the Party nor did they completely accept its doctrine, but their gravitation in that direction became the outstanding theme in their writing. It was natural that they should have to deal with such a problem. They believed that major reforms were absolutely essential, and the Marxian analysis of conditions seemed the most thorough. It recognized the growing extremes of wealth and the disturbing concentration of power in the economic world, and it offered a comprehensive solution. Thus, for those who believed that more was wrong than could be traced to individual transgressors or could be corrected by piecemeal legislation, the Socialist argument was one to be reckoned with.

Like almost all of the other muckrakers, David Graham Phillips and Lincoln Steffens moved in liberal and reform-minded circles, in which were numbered many Socialists. Phillips was greatly shaken when his intimate friend and former city editor on the *World,* Charles Edward Russell, joined the Party. Steffens, who knew almost all of the Socialist leaders, was confronted by Upton Sinclair demanding of him, "Don't you see it? Don't you see what you are showing?" Eugene V. Debs himself added, "You have written from and have been inspired by a social brain, a social heart, and a social conscience and if you are not a socialist I do not know one."[1]

The Socialists seemed alive and eager in the struggle to create a better world; it was this spirit which had such great attraction for Ray Stannard Baker and seemed compelling to Phillips and Steffens. They admired this dedication to such a cause, and if Baker had been repelled by the materialism of the rank and file, Steffens and Phillips were captivated by the selflessness of the leaders. However for all that they found much that was desirable in socialism, they had serious doubts on important matters of theory. Emphasizing the political and social aspects of society, they were ill at ease when dealing with economic problems. They seemed inclined to equate their discomfort with the rejection of the Marxist doctrine. This helped them to maintain the line that they struggled to keep between themselves and the Party, but they were ideologically as uncomfortable outside of the movement as they probably would have been within it. David Graham Phillips and Lincoln Steffens were too individualistic to have been happy within any rigid mold, but in their writing they seemed to be asking themselves the question that Steffens had asked Ida Tarbell when Charles Edward Russell joined the Socialist Party, "Is that not what we should all be doing?"[2]

Lincoln Steffens' first step in the direction was to make him famous and was an article entitled "Politics," in a series on "Great Types of Modern Business." Having seen the repeated failure of movements for covic betterment, he had come to the conclusion that reform failed because the standard remedy, a "business government," never worked. Politics, Steffens explained, had its own rules. It could not be run in the manner of any other profession. Good politics worked on a supply-and-demand basis. The best way to keep it honest was to make the people care, understand, and participate. Steffens blamed business itself for the graft in government, for the world of commerce sought the profits of vice and privilege. On the whole, however, the journalist was not trying to focus attention on the role of business as the big boodler. That was to develop later. His primary concern was the bad citizenship of the American people and their failure to understand politics. If good government was to be secured, the political mechanism must be used by an enlightened electorate. Since the bosses ruled, they had to be either purified or replaced by good government bosses. Thus Lincoln Steffens set forth in outline the factors he considered responsible for political corruption.[3] Initially, he knew little about the action of these forces. It took him almost thirteen years of writing to fill in the outline.

In *The Shame of the Cities* he began to spell out the story. Corruption came from the top. The typical citizen looked with pride on America as a business nation. The high priest of the new commercial faith, the big businessman, was the worst grafter. Steffens found him "buying boodlers in St. Louis, defending grafters in Minneapolis, originating corruption in Pittsburgh, sharing with the bosses in Philadelphia, deploring reform in Chicago, and beating good government with corruption funds in New York."[4] In order to get privileges the corporation purchased politics in a systematic fashion. As Steffens soon came to point out, the "system" extended up into the administration of the state and nation, making municipal reform almost impossible. People seemed to mind only scandal, not corruption, and reform never lasted. Occasionally there would be quarrels among the bosses, or the public would engage in a short-term revolt. Initial success for the reformers was always followed by neglect and the surrender of responsibility. The political parties only added to the trouble. As long as the mass of the citizens adhered to political labels it could be easily manipulated.

Steffens' exposés of municipal graft were overtly designed to create action by stirring up civic pride. Throughout there was a hopefully optimistic note of moral awakening. Repeatedly Steffens appealed to the common people, but paradoxically it was always the strong leader who accomplished something despite business attack and public apathy. In the series on dishonesty in state government, Steffens wrote of the need to make businessmen patriotic. His stories of achievement were always about dedicated individuals such as Jacob Riis, Tom Johnson, Joseph Folk and Robert M. La Follette. These men solved the problem of democratic leadership by rousing the citizenry to action instead of performing the tasks for it.[5] This was the basic theme of *The Upbuilders*. The country had been betrayed by the old leaders, and now it needed a new kind. In his description of such men, Steffens began to refer to his solution as "practical Christianity." It was the spirit which led the individual to consider the good of the whole community. This was real democracy. Its motivating force was love which would overcome selfishness and would be the avenue to reform and democracy. "That sounds almost Christian," he wrote, "and it isn't business."[6]

In Boston he had worked with a civic group in an effort to combine self-government with leadership. The mass of citizens was to be led by the big men of politics and business who were to be inspired by a dedication to service.[7] As Steffens had pointed out to the boss of Philadelphia, the politicians organized social treason by betraying the people whose trust they carried.[8] What a better world it could be if the natural leaders of society realized that working for the community was a bigger and more exciting enterprise than running a railroad or a gas company for private profit.

The Boston experiment had not worked because the political

and economic leaders of the city did not carry it out, and Steffens was also unsuccessful with his other try at starting at the top. In attempting to compromise the bitter antagonism between capital and labor which focused on the trial of the McNamara brothers for the Los Angeles *Times* bombing, Steffens sought to act as go-between for the defense and the business-backed prosecution. The McNamaras confessed, but instead of the expected lenient sentences and labor-management reconciliation, the brothers were sentenced to severe terms.[9]

Although Steffens would not espouse any doctrine—other than his own of applied Christianity—he found that certain institutional changes were necessary. Since privilege was a temptation to corruption, it had to be removed. The standard remedies of law enforcement and the regulation of business were not sufficient. The necessary instruments of government were not sufficiently honest and unprejudiced, and the basic evil of selfishness would still be untouched. In 1908 Steffens favored governmental ownership of public utilities. By 1914 he was talking in vague terms of taxing away unearned increment, primarily of land, and giving each man the full extent of the value that he produced.[10] How it was to be done he did not specify.

Beginning in 1908, when he announced that he was finished with muckraking and concerned with solutions,[11] Steffens moved closer to socialism. He did not join the Party and criticized important aspects of its theory, but at the same time his sympathy with its ideals and policies grew. In writing of the candidacy of Eugene V. Debs, he described the social problem as a combination of over-production and under-consumption. The markets were glutted with products which the workers, the needy and the unemployed could not afford to buy. Only the Socialists, he felt, recognized the full import of the great imbalance and offered a solution. They alone knew the joy of the common struggle and were organized to do something about it.

However, even though Steffens was completely captivated by Debs' love of mankind, he refrained from a full endorsement of the Party because of its "excesses and fallacies."[12]

The two aspects which held him back were a rather vague dislike of concentrated economic power and his strong opposition to the idea of class struggle. He could not bear to see the centralization of power in industry and finance that the Socialists believed was involved in the transition from monopoly to government ownership. Steffens was not at home on the subject of industrial evolution, and he seldom went into details. He knew men and he knew politics and government. He saw the effect of economic developments upon them, but he was never very specific about the mechanism of the productive process itself. His one attempt to describe its nature was not a success. Steffens' approach had been an attempt to carry over his political solution into the industrial world. He felt that the people should practice some form of business citizenship, perhaps with individual stockholders participating in policy determination.[13] How this difficult feat was to be accomplished he did not say.

By 1914, when he published the story of his Boston failure, economic democracy had come to mean that the workingman should realize the full value of his toil. This would not mean, he maintained—perhaps in opposition to the Socialists—the centralized concentration of power. Although he placed the blame for existing inequities on conditions rather than individuals, Steffens felt that he had escaped from doctrinaire bondage by disclaiming economic determinism. By "industrial democracy" and the equalization of opportunity through the removal of privilege, man could escape from the vise of conditions. This would lead to cultural and social heterodoxy and freedom of development. In advocating this viewpoint, Steffens seemed to believe that he was in strong disagreement with the Socialists.

Perhaps the greatest barrier to Steffens' identification with any left-wing party was his opposition to any conception of class struggle. Although many American Socialists were not strongly concerned with any such strife, Steffens felt that this aspect of the dialectic was too important to the philosophy of the movement to be ignored. In his scheme of social redemption, Steffens planned a large role for the natural leaders who had led America to a state of business domination. He put this into a paradox with which he loved to confront his more radical friends. If there was so much good in the "worst" people, must there not be some good in the "best" ones too? he asked.[14] Lincoln Steffens was a Socialist of an earlier non-Marxian variety.

During the years 1902 and 1903, David Graham Phillips wrote more than twenty articles for the *Saturday Evening Post* picturing the grasp of commercialism and corporate influence in America. Even so, he believed that industry and democracy had produced a prosperous people despite the plutocracy balanced on top.[15] His initial concern was with the influence of money on those who had it, but he soon became deeply upset over the results which touched the whole nation. The effect on the wealthy was developed most clearly in Phillips' early novels. The idle possessors of great fortunes were trying to create an American aristocracy, whose main characteristics were extravagance and ostentation. This was expressed in enormous mansions, foreign servants, the purchase of alien titles in the marriage market, snobbery, publicized philanthropy, and an insistence on artificial caste distinction. Cut off from the vital productive life of the nation, such existence was without real purpose and vulgar. It resulted in the destruction of the value in human relationships: friendship, trust, love and family.

At first Phillips attacked the men who pursued Mammon, but he soon shifted the blame to the women who worshipped the social snobbery that money purchased. Theirs was a meaningless world and they brought up their children to similar lives of vanity and uselessness; "the second generation of the rich," Phillips wrote, "is rotten with the money cancer."[16] By novel, play, and article he criticized the parasitic purposelessness of women who turned marriage into a calculated pursuit of social status, and he advocated the usefulness of divorce and the importance of sexual honesty. The vitality of a union came through a sharing and a partnership of equals. To go along with the masterful men of whom he always wrote, there was need for women of strength and integrity. In her own way the woman needed to have a creative personality in order to make her contribution.[17] The conclusion of this line of thought was Phillips' vast posthumously-published novel *Susan Lenox: Her Fall and Rise,* which was the story of a woman who finally became great through breaking all bonds of conventionality.

Initially Phillips had disliked concentrated wealth because it destroyed democratic simplicity; in a short time he came to attack it for creating undemocratic poverty. As this happened his novels shifted from social to political themes. He pictured his friend and perpetual hero, Senator Albert J. Beveridge, as well as Senators Nelson Aldrich and Mark Hanna, President William McKinley, and the New York life insurance scandals. In *The Deluge* he presented an acute fictionalized biography of Thomas W. Lawson. In his articles and books, Phillips set forth the plutocratic control of the professional (medicine and law) and the articulate (press, colleges and churches) classes of the Republic by social and economic bribery. To share in the spoils, to shake the plum tree, had become the American dream, and the access to its favors was controlled by the political boss.[18]

Central to this picture was the encroachment of the plutocracy on all branches of government: the courts, the Administration, the Congress, and especially the Senate of the United

States. At the behest of William Randolph Hearst, he wrote a set of articles for *Cosmopolitan* on the corruption of the upper Chamber.[19] Although this series was the occasion for President Roosevelt's characterization of the "muckrakers,"[20] Phillips' effort was no wild polemic. Rather, it was a factually presented indictment of the role of wealth in the highest legislative body of the nation.

Phillips began each article with the Constitutional definition: "Treason against the United States shall consist only in levying war against them, or in *adhering to their enemies, giving them aid and comfort.*" He did not maintain that a large portion of the Senate was actually venal although five members were under indictment and others had been similarly accused. However, they owed their allegiance to the money power, rather than to the people whom they were supposed to represent. The greatest hold that the "interests" had was that they financed the Parties. Would the plutocracy supply the funds if they were to receive nothing in return? Senator Aldrich was "Boss" of the Senate because he was the representative of all of the interests. Arthur P. Gorman, the Democratic minority leader, was his right-hand man. Most of the Senators were lawyers, as were the state legislators who elected them. Almost all were eager for retainers from the big corporations, especially the railroads. The friends and acquaintances of the man in public life were drawn from the "exploiting" class. From these alliances he too often developed a misplaced sense of loyalty. The result was that wealth and power were put in the hands of a few, primarily by the failure of Congress to safeguard the people with necessary laws. This lack of suitable regulatory legislation was the basic factor in Phillips' analysis of plutocratic growth. The two best indications of the treason of big business against the American nation, he wrote, were to be found in tariff and in railway legislation. These were the chief ways in which "the interests" fattened upon the American people.

Although alarmed by the power and—to a lesser degree—
by the results of the plutocracy, Phillips continually reaffirmed
his belief in democracy and its two keys, education and the
suffrage. In *The Reign of Gilt,* published in 1905, he had set
forth the reasons for this faith. He believed that aristocracy and
caste were the natural results of widespread ignorance and that
democracy was the inevitable outcome of growing intelligence.
Education was, for him, "democracy's dynamo." However he
questioned the freedom of the universities, especially those of
the East which his novels pilloried as snob factories swayed by
the pressures of plutocratic philanthropy. The Middle West, he
believed, was a healthier society.

While learning nourished the wisdom that was the raw material of progress, science and industrialism were creating a new
political fluidity which would undermine the political bosses. At
the same time, through increasing productivity, they were raising the standard of living. The immigrant was also a revitaliz-
ing stream in the democratic life. Those who came had believed so strongly in freedom that they crossed the oceans to
seek it were a conscious, determined and dedicated force against
oppression and aristocracy. The growing pressure of concentrated wealth was making the citizenry increasingly discontented;
reactionary and aristocratic ideals had not caught on. In writing
of the senatorial "treason" Phillips did not lose his belief in the
inevitability of democracy. This faith remained with him
throughout his life, but as he continued to write, he changed
his conception of the nature of democracy.

At first he saw it as the treasured possession of the restless
middle class. Socialism abroad, he maintained, was not radical
but very much an approximation of the ideals of the American
Republic. The "revolution" of which he frequently wrote would
be caused not by mob rule but by mis-rule. It would be the
result of bourgeois discontent rather than proletarian unrest.[21]

The only way to end corruption, he felt, was for the government to take over such utilities as the railroads. Regulation had been worse than useless. On some occasions he was willing to call this step socialistic, but he usually avoided any labels. Although he praised the Socialists for seeing and grappling with the real issues of the distribution of wealth, he objected to their dogmatism. They were far too precise, he complained; their formulations were too much like prophecy. His principal motivation seemed to be that he felt himself uncomfortably close to their point of view and sought to avoid becoming so identified.[22] As he came nearer to the Marxian doctrines in the last years of his life, Phillips refrained from any mention of socialism. In his two most radical novels, the term is never used.

With *The Second Generation* in 1907 Phillips centered his efforts on his novels. In this book, which many critics considered his best, he set forth a socialist panacea. No longer interested in the virtues of the bourgeoisie, he had worked out a theory of surplus value to show how a parasitic society robbed the toiler of his labor. The author's hero was a workingman who stuck by his class and refused to become a foreman because he couldn't "speed" the men: "Did you ever think, it takes one of us only about a day to make enough barrels to pay his week's wages, and that he has to donate the other five days' work for the privilege of being allowed to live? If I rose I'd be living off those five days of stolen labor."[23] In Phillips' utopia, "profits" would be abolished and industry turned over to the workers in a gradually cumulative process. Factories were to be forced out of business by non-dividend-paying competition and taken over by the toilers. Phillips did not postulate transition from giant private to public trusts, for neither monopoly nor the national government seemed to be involved in this shop-by-shop process. When the change of ownership had been accomplished, the workers and their families would respond to their improved circumstances by learning to use their new leisure instead of merely existing to labor long hours for others.

Culture was unproductive in the hands of the rich, he wrote, and meaningful only in those of the workers.

The analysis did not, however, absorb Phillips' full attention. The novels which he wrote between *The Second Generation* and his sudden death in 1911[24] usually dealt with the problems of marriage, divorce, and the range of man-woman relations and made no reference to his labor theories. However his post-humously published *The Conflict* plunged heavily into a disser-tation on labor and on class divisions. The former was too powerful to be kept down while the latter were too strong to be crossed even by his hitherto omnipotent heroes and heroines. As an ideological manifesto, it was a bad book—or perhaps one which Phillips himself had not finished. It opposed strikes be-cause they gave the capitalists an excuse to resort to force. He maintained that labor could prevail peacefully, but the book was not explicit about either the process or the results of power. The solidarity which it preached somehow looked more like an end than a means. The basic element of the book was a polemic emphasizing class conflict in vaguely Marxian terms.

This was not presented naked and unwashed, however, but only after having been bathed in the blood of the lamb. Along with his creation of a messianic hero—carpenter and son of a carpenter—Phillips had his heroine eulogize a Christ-like Karl Marx: "And they were both labor leaders—labor agitators. The first proclaimed the brotherhood of man. But he regarded this world as hopeless and called on the weary and heavy-laden masses to look to the next world for the righting of their wrongs. Then—eighteen centuries after—came the second Jew—and he said 'No! not in the hereafter, but in the here. Here and now, my brothers. Let us make this world a heaven. Let us redeem ourselves and destroy this devil of ignorance who is holding us in this hell! It was three hundred years before the first Jew began to triumph. It won't be so long before there are monu-ments to Marx in clean and beautiful and free cities all over the earth.' " The moving force of change set forth in *The Conflict* was the socialist spirit, analysis and movement, devoid of force and violence. It was moving toward an inevitable triumph within the democratic framework.[25]

While Lincoln Steffens and David Graham Phillips successfully avoided casting their lots with the Socialists, Charles Edward Russell and Upton Sinclair came to believe that socialism was the only effective way to achieve the better society which all of the muckrakers desired.

🕸 9 🕸

SOCIALISM:

UPTON SINCLAIR

AND CHARLES EDWARD RUSSELL

The first decade of the twentieth century was the "golden age" of the American Socialists. Their campaign train, "The Red Special," brought the fiery words of Eugene V. Debs to the cities and prairies. They elected their first Congressmen and hundreds of municipal officials. Upton Sinclair organized an Inter-collegiate Socialist Society; there was a growing radical press, and the Party was influential in academic and journalistic circles. The muckrakers felt that they lived in a period of crisis and great change. Socialism promised action and both Upton Sinclair and Charles Edward Russell were drawn by the idea of imminent revolutionary changes—perhaps within the decade.

Much of Upton Sinclair's life was a struggle to become a great author. Throughout his early years he suffered from the combined pressures of financial and emotional insecurity and depression. He was beset by every conceivable misfortune of poverty, lack of recognition, and ill health. He felt trapped by puritanical torment and frustration stemming from the opposition of his in-laws, inability to support his wife, incompatibility, an unwanted child, and a period of enforced celibacy for fear of having another. He poured all of his experience and longings into his writing. Although his problems continued and multiplied with success, it was under the spur of these conditions that he turned out his initial books and articles, and that he was converted to socialism.[1]

In the autumn of 1902, Upton Sinclair had met a number of the socialist intelligentsia including George D. Herron. They were attracted to him, and Herron subsidized and influenced l. m toward socialism. It was a quick conversion, for Sinclair w..s by temperament an extremist, completely bound up in an ideological approach to society. His friend Floyd Dell pointed out that "His scientific interests, his acceptance of the Darwinian ideas of evolution, his repudiation of the church and of mysticism, his interest in history and belief in the democratic ideal, his sense of justice and abhorrence of a class society, his utopian tendencies, his conception of himself as a radical and revolutionist, had half prepared him for the new philosophy of Socialism." This conversion forced Sinclair to turn outside of himself for values, and thus, to a degree, he escaped from the sense of isolation and introspection which had been the essence of his approach to artistic creativity.[2]

His conversion to socialism offered more than a cause and an explanation of society to the young author. In reviewing one of his own books for the *Independent*, he explained that this was part of the wave of the future. "In the joyous day when the impending revolution shall have consummated itself and the soul of man is free . . ." he wrote, the artist would be the sole critic of his own creations. After all, who knew better what they were about.[3] Sinclair now turned his back on his former belief in pure aesthetics in literature, which he maintained had no vitality to withstand bourgeois degradation. Revolution was the prerequisite of art.

As befitted a newly won convert, Upton Sinclair was busy during the fall of 1904 explaining to everyone what he had discovered. He campaigned for the Party and lectured to strikers in Chicago, telling them that they had to use the ballot to seek political power; then they could establish worker ownership. Once they received the full value of what they produced, all the evils of society—robbery, corruption, unemployment, prostitution, drunkenness, war, idleness and hard times—would be no more.[4]

Sinclair's philosophy was a blend characteristic of American socialism. It combined typical Marxian analysis of the economic ills with a personalized mixture of solutions. The United States, Sinclair felt, was undergoing the last stage of a long evolutionary process. The concentration of wealth had become so great that a revolution was in the offing. The masses would starve unless they rose and took over. The principle form of pressure that shaped society was "the surplus" and this held a central role in Sinclair's ideology. Through the maldistribution which created it, capital outstripped its investment opportunities, for the people did not have the money to buy their own production.

The revolutionary transition would begin in the United States and spread peacefully from the more advanced to the backward areas. Sinclair was never quite consistent about whether or not the Socialist Party would actually have to be voted into power before this would be accomplished, but he was sure that political pressure alone could do it.[5] There would be no confiscation of personal property. All that a person used himself would be his own. The Party simply wished to end private control of that which ought to be public. Rent, profits, interest and dividends should belong to all. Since capital equipment could not be redistributed, it had to be owned by the nation itself. In answer to the high priest of Spencerian *laissez-faire,* William Graham Sumner, Sinclair claimed to be the idealistic believer in Christian ends. Sumner, he maintained, was the materialist. Jesus, Sinclair contended, was an agitator, anarchist, and workingman—

the first socialist. Like many other muckrakers, the young writer considered Christ's teachings a basically radical force which had been corrupted by wealth and the churches.[6]

Upton Sinclair's major work, *The Jungle,* was a broadly written socialist manifesto which its author felt to be the beginning of proletarian literature in America. Into it he wrote not only the results of his observations in Chicago but much of the story of his spiritual and physical sufferings. The unhappy, never really free, marriage of Jurgis and Oona was his own, and the exhortation which ended the book was one which Sinclair had actually made to the strikers. On his broad canvas he centered the picture of the treatment of the immigrant in the United States. America was no land of opportunity for those unfortunates who were deliberately imported to overcrowd the labor market and to break strikes. They were compelled to struggle against being replaced by the machines or undercut by child labor. The worker was powerless against the system under which the beef trust owned both him and the law. The lot of the immigrant was the disruption of his family and the destruction of all of the vestiges of civilized life. Sinclair's hero, Jurgis, was a powerful man of immense physical strength and will, who fell before a system that was stronger than any individual. Only the Socialists could successfully combat it, Sinclair wrote, for they understood the trusts and would take them over rather than destroy them. The Party was the expression of the desire of the people to survive, and in Packingtown he saw its rising tide. Socialism was on the move, he exulted, and with the growth of radical democracy the old parties would be shown up. "Chicago," he chanted, "will be ours."[7]

Once the evils caused by competition and industrial warfare were abolished, all individual and social ills would also be removed. War would be inconceivable; there would be no temptation to drink, and no more waste through parasitical trades and occupations such as the house servant, the milliner, advertising and multiple retail outlets. The machinery of civil law would be unnecessary, and slums and disease would be a thing of the past. Sinclair poured a potpourri of remedies into his reborn society. Insurance would be supplied by the government. Agriculture would be run on more scientific and efficient principles leading to nutritious living, which, to Sinclair's unhappy digestive system, suggested vegetarianism.

His picture of the Socialist utopia bore a strong resemblance to Edward Bellamy's *Looking Backward,* of which the muckraker wrote glowingly in *The Industrial Republic.* Sinclair found the formula for this reborn society in the socialist dictum of "communism in material production, anarchism in intellectual." With the abolition of privilege and exploitation, each man could be given the means to live in accordance with his labor and otherwise be left free.[8]

However, although he believed that the new order would mean complete freedom for the individual, Sinclair was too absorbed in the socialist ideology to conceive of anyone's living independently of the group. Foreshadowing his own experiment in that field, he dilated on the positive economies of communal living. He invested the money from the phenomenal sale of *The Jungle* in just such a venture. His "Home Colony" on the palisades of New Jersey was to be a cooperative hotel, composed of a group of people who wanted to run their domestic affairs in a more scientific manner. Although his colony need not be a party cell, the inhabitants had to be at least in sympathy with the movement if democratic principles were to work. He later reminisced about his ill-fated effort as being "the industrial Republic in the making." People had lived there because they wanted to, but someday everyone would have to. Such was the nature of the freedom he sought.[9] This paradox of regimented freedom arising from communal living was one of the most indicative characteristics of Sinclair's nature. He was so wrapped up in the Socialist Party that life outside of it had no meaning. Few people had been more alone and had waged so desperate a battle to belong. He had had to stand by himself too much and his sense of duty and mission were too strong to picture freedom as being equivalent to any such individualism.

The Jungle was an immediate though controversial success. Despite this, it failed completely in its purpose of winning people to socialism. Sinclair's interest in correcting the revolting methods by which meat was prepared for human consumption was only an incidental theme. He intended to draw attention to the plight of the immigrant and workingman, but in this his bolt missed its mark. In the widespread public indignation over impure food, the desperate state of the inhabitants of Packingtown went almost unnoticed. "I aimed at the public's heart," he wrote, "and by accident I hit it in the stomach."[10]

However, having created a national sensation by this revelation of conditions in the slaughterhouses, he turned his attention to substantiating and publicizing his discoveries. He was invited to lunch at the White House, and ran, unsuccessfully, for the United States Senate from New Jersey. He supported the meat inspection bill sponsored by Senator Albert J. Beveridge, but maintained that there would always be danger until a municipal slaughterhouse system was established.[11]

Returning to his original theme of the exploitation of the working classes, he next set out to do a series on child labor. In order to avoid the tangent which had arisen in the case of *The Jungle,* he picked the glass-blowing industry because there was no problem of the preparation of food. However, the study was not published and served only to confirm his conviction that capitalism prevented the spread of the truth about industrial conditions and that he particularly was harassed by a captive press. The following year he again felt thwarted when the *American* did not print his story of the Wall Street panic of 1907.[12]

Despite his disappointments and frustrations, Sinclair did not despair. His major treatise on the future of society, *The Industrial Republic,* was strongly optimistic. Drawing upon his previous writings and a plethora of other works on socialism and economic problems, he hailed the coming revolution. His proof of both its inevitability and its imminence stemmed from his belief in social evolution. With the development of a favorable balance of trade, which was the result of the over-production of capital, the United States was entering the final stage of capitalist decline. The growth of trusts was but another sign. To the search for foreign markets, he ascribed imperialism and foreign wars; on the trusts fell the blame for the increasing misery of the workers.

The purpose of his book, Sinclair explained, was to prove that the evolutionary force of industrial competition had done its job. Now the trusts, those "marvelous industrial machines," would be turned to serve the good of all. Competition would be transferred from the economic sphere to that of intellectual activity and the general benefit of society. A joint international effort to aid backward countries would replace imperialism. All activities such as art and religion would be supported by the people who wanted them, and so there would be no regulation or censorship.[13]

The moment was always just around the corner. Not a patient man, Sinclair had little use for a future that would not take place in the present. In 1904, he had predicted a growing strength of radicalism as the result of increasing unemployment. In two years the Party's membership would be between two and three million, "and within six months after the Presidential election of 1908 the American people will have the Socialist programme in full operation." In *The Jungle,* he felt constrained to push the date back to 1912, but in *The Industrial Republic* he offered a more exact timetable. Sinclair's white hope was William Randolph Hearst. Pledged to put an end to class government, he would be the Democratic candidate. The nation would be racked by unemployment, strikes, bloodshed and a growing agitation led by the Socialists. The Republican standard bearer, Theodore Roosevelt, would be forced to accept radicalism. Nevertheless, Hearst would win, and the creation of the "Industrial Republic" would begin.[14]

However, as the 1912 election approached, Sinclair made no further mention of it, and there was a change in the tone of his writing as well. His faith in socialism had not been weakened, but he had come to realize that the period of preparation and propaganda would be a long one. In his *Plays of Protest* he was willing to talk about the great change, but Russia, not the United States, was to be its predestined location. In rewriting his Wagnerian phantasy, *Prince Hagen,* he described an uprising provoked by the limitless greed of the rich, but it had no promise of belonging to the near future.

Upton Sinclair's best statement of his changed attitude after 1907 was his description of "The Muckrake Man" for the *Independent.* "As a rule," he explained, "the Muckrake Man began his career with no theories, as a simple observer of facts known to every person at all 'on the inside' of business and politics. But he followed the facts, and the facts always led him to one conclusion; until he finally discovered to his consternation that he was enlisted in a revolt against capitalism."[15] Sinclair himself had never been content to be a "simple observer" and, on the whole, had followed a somewhat reversed order.

The revolt against a competitive, business society which made Charles Edward Russell into a muckraker and led him into the ranks of the Socialist Party was peculiarly American. He was exaggerating when he wrote in his autobiography that "It was true that I had never read *Das Kapital* and could not have told Karl Marx from Frederick Engels if I had met them walking arm in arm up the street. Few persons can be conceived to have known less about Scientific Socialism."[16] Although he blamed a doctrinal villain, "the surplus," for all ininternational conflict, most of his ideas seem to come from his own experience with and a basic sympathy for the underdog. Unlike the writings of Upton Sinclair, Russell's do not contain reference to socialist writers and thinkers.

Russell's philosophy bore the imprint of most of the reform movements of his times. His grandfather had been an ardent prohibitionist in England, and his father carried on the family tradition in the United States with a firm stand against slavery and the tariff. As a student Russell was an admirer of the great agnostic Robert G. Ingersoll, and read the writings of Henry Demarest Lloyd and Henry George. His life-long hero was the abolitionist turned social critic, Wendell Phillips. Russell was strongly influenced by Arthur Latham Perry's political economy textbook which blamed the tariff for the evils of accumulated wealth. This theory seemed to explain the depressed state of agriculture, and so in 1881 Russell helped to found the Iowa State Free Trade League, later becoming an officer of the national organization. Russell's interest soon shifted from the tariff to corporate power in general. For this he gave credit to General James Baird Weaver, the perennial Greenback candidate, who taught him that power over transportation, not the tariff, was the grestest menace to the Republic. This message was reinforced by the experience of Russell's father who had lost his newspaper for opposing the power of the railroads. Through the era of the muckrakers, Russell's writings seldom strayed far away from the connection between monopoly in transportation and the concentration of wealth.[17]

As a newspaperman, Russell had seen poverty abroad and at home. A single Taxer for a while, he joined the Populist movement in its last days, and took part in various reform movements in New York City. He served under William Randolph Hearst, whose defense of labor and the underdog he echoed and praised in his own writings.[18] In 1905 he was asked by *Everybody's* to arrange for an article on a trust prosecution in Chicago. The result was his muckrake career which ultimately produced more than a hundred and fifty articles and a number of books, and resulted in his nomination as Socialist candidate for some of the highest offices in the land.

His initial series was an account of how the Beef Trust had parlayed rebates and a refrigerator car monopoly into an empire of measureless riches and influence. It had finally reached the point where it owned "factories, shops, stockyards, mills, land and land companies, plants, warehouses, politicians, legislators and Congressmen." Because it controlled the prices that people paid for food, he wrote vividly, "Three times a day, this power comes to the table of every household in America." The fault lay in the false set of values of a society which believed in the survival of the fittest and deified success. This philosophy meant "the right of the strong to annihilate the weak, the theory that in business any advantage is fair—the accepted creed of inordinate gain."[19] What was needed was a changed morality that would establish standards of public service. Greater direct participation by the people in political affairs would end the rule of the bosses. An honest determination to enforce the laws would destroy special privilege and monopoly.

Soon afterwards *Everybody's* sent Russell on a trip around the world to gather facts about social movements. When he came back he was a socialist, although it took him several years to actually join the Party. Wherever he went, he had seen the combined forces of caste and business power on top. Artificial barriers divided mankind, enforcing the subjugation of the lower classes and making poverty inescapable. He particularly disliked England, as had David Graham Phillips, which he accused of being the fountainhead of caste. The "normal ties of sympathy and good-will between men" could not exist in such an atmosphere. Such evils revenged themselves upon the whole of society, for the "pariah breeds influenza in the East End of London and the plague in the purlieus of Bombay."[20] One theme that never changed and continued to repeat itself in Russell's writing was the cost of poverty and misery to the countries that permitted them.

When he gathered together his ideas in "The Soldiers of the Common Good," he had come to attribute all hopeful signs of social progress to "the idea of state interference, which . . . has become a recognized and vital function of government."[21] Great Britain and the United States were the prime examples of nations in which an industrial aristocracy was uncurbed by governmental regulation. However, without considering the question of freedom, he singled out Germany and Japan as the revolutionists of the age. Both of them were achieving tremendous economic power and efficiency through the activity of the central government. They would soon challenge the position of the faltering, trustified, Anglo-Saxon nations, he warned. Among the latter only Australia and New Zealand showed promise.

"Always heretofore government has given the greatest share of its attention to those that least needed it," he explained. Now there were encouraging signs all over the world that henceforth government would turn its attention to the weak and unfortunate. The United States, he seemed confident, would find the way out through the growth of political and industrial democracy. One thing, though, had become certain: regulation was not possible and public ownership was the only way in which predatory interests could be kept in check.[22]

In 1907 and 1908 Russell wrote on the wealth of Trinity Church, prison conditions, elections purchasing, and the transit system of New York City. His thesis was always that wealth came from exploitation, not service. Despite this familiar attack on the corporations these articles contained a surprising absence of ideological comment. However, Russell appears to have been engaged in serious reflection, for in October of 1908 he applied for membership in the Socialist Party. Singling out poverty and slum conditions as the outstanding problems, he declared that he was convinced of the futility of any other remedy. His view of socialism was essentially humanistic. It was born of sympathy for the suffering of men and from his hatred of the poverty which, he believed, was unjustly forced upon them. The text for his philosophy was: "Inasmuch as ye have done it to the least of my brethren ye have done it unto me." In an interview for *Human Life,* he declared that "so long as the slum exists there is no other question worth considering than its obliteration."[23] Because the Socialists seemed to have the only real solution and were the loudest voice of protest against social injustice, he turned to them. His desire to end the effects of poverty was the principal theme of his apologia, *Why I am a Socialist,* published in 1910.

With Russell's conversion his analysis became set. The trust was simply an inevitable phase of evolution. Consolidation occurred because it provided the most economical base for production. However, as long as it was in private hands, the savings would go to the few. The trusts would continue to interfere with the government and public honesty in order to ensure the continued enjoyment of their spoils. They were, however, preparing the way for socialism. The evolution from competition to monopoly seemed self-evident to Russell. He devoted greater attention to showing why the process of change had to continue on to the cooperative commonwealth. Although economic concentration was an improvement, it was still inevitably subject to waste and mismanagement, and was operated at a tremendous social cost. "Sometimes, to Trust extortion," he explained, "are added Trust interference with public affairs and Trust corruption of politics.[24]

A sizable portion of Russell's writing between 1908 and

1914 was devoted to the elucidation of those three categories. The essential characteristic of the extortion was the rising cost of living caused by stock watering and over-capitalization. This was the real story of the looted traction systems of the American cities and of the building of the great railroads.

Interference with public affairs went beyond the level of corruptly buying franchises and special privileges. The "interests" controlled the national supply of money and credit and thus were in a stronger position than the government itself. The unconsumed surplus—which became one of Russell's major ideological preoccupations—needed outlets. Because of the concentration of wealth in the hands of a few, the domestic market did not suffice. The results were imperialism and war. "For all times, and in all places, and under all conditions, Capitalism is War," he thundered, using the outbreaks in Spanish Morocco and the Boer War as examples of the pressure of interest payments and imperialistic investments.[25] Later, on the eve of World War I, he wrote that "for the high purpose of finding a dumping ground abroad for a surplus domestic product, capitalists force wars. Then under the guise of 'Patriotism' the workers of one country are fooled into going to the front in defense of their Nation's honor. There they murder in battle the workers of another country."[26]

The trust corruption of politics was the simplest and most familiar of his themes. "Privilege (otherwise called franchises) and public contracts are the source of this fortune-making," he explained. "In America privilege is obtained in only one way, and that is by some form of political corruption."[27] His studies of the railroads, municipal government, election practices, and great fortunes all repeated this story.

In a series of articles in *Success* Russell ventured an analysis which tied the threads together. There was an aura of unreality about the omnipotence which he attributed to trust, interest, and class. Did they actually exercise quite the degree of power or unity of purpose of which they were accused? Russell explained that his favorite targets, accumulated wealth and the corporations, were but symptoms of the all-pervading spirit of commercialism in American life. It was not so much the trust in particular, as the business outlook and spirit in general.

By the beginning of the twentieth century, Business assumed the responsibility of feeding, sheltering, and clothing the American people. It was natural that this mechanism would be the primal force in society and would become the government. It was hypocrisy to refuse to acknowlege this, and the absence of recognition obliged Business to indulge in illegal and subterranean methods in order to gain support from politics and the press. The public refused to accept the industrial and commercial interests as the most important element in the land and sought to impose foolish regulations and restrictions. In return, Business bought newspapers whose support it should have had anyway, and allied itself with caste, vice, graft, and crime, always opposing liberal and enlightened movements.

By these activities, Business acted unwisely in seeking immediate short-run gains. In the long run it destroyed itself by assuming a bad name and creating an unhealthy atmosphere and physical conditions. "Business is too big, too important, too broad, too national," Russell protested, "to entertain class prejudices."[28] Increasing poverty limited the domestic market and sapped the national stamina. People without money could not buy goods. The worst enemy of continued profits was the slum, and yet unenlightened Business fostered the growth of general misery and poverty. Eventually, he warned, the result would be bloody revolution. The force which pushed business into a self-ruinous course was the huge increase in capitalization. The resulting pressure for profits was too strong to permit business to recognize and follow its own true interests. Further evolution, Russell believed, had become inevitable.

Russell was the Socialist candidate for governor of New York in 1910 and 1912, for mayor of New York City in 1913, and for the United States Senate the following year. He delivered numerous speeches, helped found the National Association for the Advancement of Colored People, and was co-editor with A. M. Simons of a Socialist weekly, *The Coming Nation*. Even so, he continued to write for *Cosmopolitan, Hampton's* and *Pearson's*. He was a muckraker at heart and it was from this feeling that his socialism rose, rather than the reverse as was the case with Upton Sinclair.

Russell believed that the time of crisis was at hand. Socialism was on the march everywhere. The transition from private to publicly owned trusts was about to take place. Turning to American history, he drew a parallel with the nation at the outbreak of the Civil War. There was the same rule of caste and "interests," the same growing moral protests, and the same dissolution of the old parties.[29] In contrast to Upton Sinclair, he was far more concerned with the stage from which mankind was to escape than with drawing a picture of the future. Business would be run for the common good, and that was enough. He hoped that by the abolition of the profit motive and the pressures of competition, all forms of strife and oppression among men could be ended. The adjustment of production to consumption would prevent the evils of poverty and war.[30]

By 1912 he had lost his faith in an easy and immediate victory. There was no further talk of the impending triumph. With the Party facing the prospect of a long struggle, he warned that, in seeking ultimate goals, it must scorn compromise. In 1910 he had hailed the political triumph of the Party in winning the municipal elections in Milwaukee. By the spring of 1912 he probably would not have been so certain that piecemeal electoral success was desirable. If Socialism was to "go into the dirty game of practical politics, seeking success by compromise and bargain . . . it would inevitably fall into the pit that has engulfed all other parties," he wrote.[31]

Since he assumed that socialism was the natural outcome of popular awareness of the true nature of existing conditions, he was naturally concerned about the forces affecting public opinion. It was significant, therefore, that as his confidence in the approach of the millennium faded, there was an increasing attack upon the "corruption" of the press and education.[32] Between 1912 and 1914 even the railroads yielded first place as his favorite topic.

His disappointment and his new conception of the role of the Party brought a growing emphasis on strikes and the working class. The better life would have to be the result of a conscious, prolonged struggle. To be sure, evolution still took place, but more slowly, and there was much that needed to be done to aid its functioning. Where before he had placed his reliance for change on no chosen class, in the last prewar years Russell swung more and more toward a proletarian emphasis. In 1914 he wrote, for the first time, that only working class government would bring the co-operative commonwealth.[33]

Charles Edward Russell had become a Socialist because of the compassion he felt for the victims which he believed that society sacrificed to greed. When it seemed that competition, moral pressure, and law enforcement were not sufficient to curb the evil, his investigations led him to state ownership as the remedy. Because the Socialists manifested a sympathy and spirit similar to his own and were fighting for the same remedy, he became one of them. His belief in evolution and his long experience with the failure of tariff and regulatory actions seemed to buttress the soundness of his move. His conversion added the concept of "the surplus" to his thinking about the causes of poverty and war. It tied together his reformist ideas by explaining the "why" of the economic mechanism. According to his philosophy, the nation was then obviously ripe for the new evolutionary stage to which so many signs pointed. The political confusion, insurgency, and popular unrest fitted into an historical pattern which promised the birth of a better world. That it did not take place was extremely disappointing to him, although he did not quite admit that anything had really failed to happen. It just had not happened yet.

❦ 10 ❦

THE CELESTIAL CROWN

Lincoln Steffens told in his autobiography of accepting a challenge to prove that his home town of Greenwich, Connecticut,
was typically corrupt. While he spoke, his assistant, Walter
Lippmann, drew on a blackboard a diagram of the dishonest
functioning of government in the average American city. Then
with the help of the audience, Steffens filled in the names of the
Greenwich exemplars.[1] According to the traditional depiction
of them, the muckrakers functioned like this, writing in the
names of grafters on a ready-made chart. This interpretation,
however, misses the real spirit and importance of the movement.
The difficulty in understanding the muckrakers results from the
nature of their crusade and the way it developed. The participants were journalists, not academicians or legislators. Their
work was adapted to the medium of the popular magazines and
tended to develop in installment fashion. Few of the writers
initially began with a broad analysis of the national ills. They
started with a particular city or industry and built up a picture
of the nation as a whole, article by article, series by series. Each
crystalized his philosophy before the end of the era of exposés.

Nevertheless, the readers' initial impression of naivete and lack of direction was often the one that remained.[2]

Theodore Roosevelt's label of "muck-rakers" entrenched this popular reaction by creating a simplified picture of aimless and often unjustified sensationalism. Though the people read and absorbed the message of these journalists, the stereotype stuck. But the effect of the President's phrase was not only upon the general public but also the writers themselves. Although Charles Edward Russell, Upton Sinclair, Thomas Lawson, and Alfred Henry Lewis gloried in the title, David Graham Phillips and Ida Tarbell were extremely upset,[3] and Phillips soon gave up the magazines in order to concentrate on his novels. Some writers seem partially to have accepted T. R.'s criticism. The time came soon afterwards when Lincoln Steffens announced that he was done with exposés. "Now solutions," he proclaimed,[4] although he had been so engaged all along.

The fact that the movement was educational, rather than legislative, adds an additional difficulty to understanding the era. The journalists, agreeing upon a common enemy, wished specific reforms and often whole programs of correction, but most of them did not feel that they were in a position to lead a political movement. Rather, they set themselves to creating an informed public opinion that would make progress possible.

The muckrakers were not intent on keeping aloof from political affairs. Charles Edward Russell and Upton Sinclair were hardy campaigners on the Socialist ticket. G. K. Turner testified in crime and vice investigations. Ray Stannard Baker soon gave up his anti-political ideas, took part in local politics in Michigan, and later became a campaign adviser to Robert M. La Follette. Lincoln Steffens was involved in practically every stirring of municipal and state reform.

There can be little doubt of the journalists' earnestness and sense of dedication. Russell's muckrake convictions led him to join the Socialist Party. Tne letters and diaries of Lincoln Steffens, Ida Tarbell, Ray Stannard Baker, and David Graham Phillips showed how their hopes for the good which they might do became the central force in their lives. Although this ego-involvement was responsible for Tom Lawson's flights of fancy, for the others it meant that their effectiveness depended on a high standard of honesty and integrity. This feeling was demonstrated when the top writers on *McClure's* resigned rather than be a party to S.S. McClure's speculative experiments.

But much more was involved in the movement than the seriousness of its participants. The muckrakers presented affirmative creeds, ranging from G. K. Turner's belief that big business should be released from the trammels of laws designed for a bygone competitive economy, to the socialism of Upton Sinclair and Charles Edward Russell. All of the writers realised that vast changes had taken place in the land. More than any other group they made the people aware of what twentieth-century America was like. Quickly passing over the fields which had concerned previous generations of reformers, they evidenced little interest in currency or civil service improvements. Although they all attacked the tariff, only Ida Tarbell believed that it was a vital national problem. For the belated nineteenth-century answer to the growth of monopoly, the Sherman Anti-trust Act, there was only minority support.

Despite the diversity of their remedial views, all of the muckrakers laid the evils of society to the rise of new economic conditions. The journalists used a variety of terms: the "interests," "the System," high or frenzied finance, plutocracy, industrial aristocracy, the trusts and monopoly. In one way or another the writers were talking about the same thing. The specific agent in the national orgy of corruption was the corporations. Their highest utility, Ray Stannard Baker wrote, was that they enabled "reputable people to participate in the profits of disreputable business enterprises without disturbing their moral complacency."[5] It was just this popular indifference and acquiescence that the muckrakers tried to upset. They attempted to educate the people to the realization, as Will Irwin stated it, that "the crime of stealing the means of production through corrupt legislatures and corrupt market manipulations is as great and heinous, doubtless, as the crime of stealing silver spoons from the safe of a wealthy burgher."[6] The fault was not in the corporate form itself but rather the use to which it was being put. The moral development of the nation failed to keep pace with an enormous material expansion. The profit motive, they pointed out, had been enthroned in America. They all believed that "Business" had become the ruling force in society and, with the exception of G. K. Turner, they did not like the results. Lincoln Steffens summed it up when he wrote that "Business, the mere machinery of living, has become in America the purpose of life, the end to which all other goods—honour, religion, politics, men, women and children, the very nation itself—are sacrificed."[7]

Muckraking then, despite its gaudy show of accusations, was not directed toward seeking out individuals as scapegoats. The emphasis on prominent men as exemplification of evil was a matter of journalistic style rather than ideology. Although the muckrakers were concerned with the need for leadership, it rarely approached becoming a cult. Only Lincoln Steffens and Thomas Lawson seriously relied upon a theory of leadership. Lawson's messiah was himself, while Steffens looked to the outstanding men of business and politics to arouse a general sense of dedication to public service.

The disinclination of the journalists to tie their movement to the political chariot of any particular man in public life emerged clearly from the body of their writing. To most of them, Theodore Roosevelt initially promised the best chance for a great national readjustment. Alfred Henry Lewis and Will Irwin never faltered in their admiration, but the others became disillusioned with the President. His friends, Ray Stannard Baker and Lincoln Steffens, who held the highest hopes for him, were the most disappointed. He was, they came to believe, unconcerned about economic problems and hopelessly a trimmer. By the time most of the writers crystalized their ideas, they discovered that the Rough-rider from Oyster Bay had been left behind.

The muckrakers had no greater faith in the political parties than in outstanding individuals. Almost all of them rejected the standard national solutions of replacing the "ins" with the "outs," or "bad" with "good" government. Even the minority of Democrats among the journalists were not willing to claim that a shift in political power would in any way change conditions. Steffens, Lewis, Baker, Russell and Phillips repeatedly wrote that "Business" ruled in both parties. Nevertheless, few of the journalists became radicals. Only Charles Edward Russell was led to socialism during the muckrake era by the conviction that the traditional channels were hopeless. Upton Sinclair was already there before he turned to muckraking.

Corruption of politics was but one example of the failure of the traditional ways of doing things. Wherever the muckrakers looked they found that the national institutions no longer served the people. Politics, the law, education, the press, and religion had been diverted from their intended function and were, in varying degrees, the captive creatures of wealth. C. P. Connolly devoted his attention to the judiciary, but all the writers commented repeatedly on the failure of the courts to dispense justice. David Graham Phillips was the most concerned with the way the titans of industry corrupted the colleges with their gifts, but Ida Tarbell and the others also attacked what they considered to be false benevolence. Will Irwin made the fullest study of the press in an age of commercialism, but all were concerned with what seemed its vanishing freedom. Many of the muckrakers were particularly upset by the conservatism of organized religion. They felt that most of the churches had lost their social message and were seeking to make the people content with the world as it was, rather than inspiring them to create a better one.

Despite the growing aggregation of wealth and the inability of the country's institutions to protect the interests of the common man, the muckrakers were not prophets of gloom. All believed that the evils could be corrected and that the moment of crisis was at hand. Only Will Irwin and G. K. Turner felt that no action was necessary. To everyone, except Lawson and perhaps Turner, America meant the promise of a freer and more equalitarian land. They saw the story of the nation's march toward that goal as a dialectic process by which every struggle against a newly rising wave of reaction resulted in a new advance for the people. Both Baker and Phillips wrote of such waves, and Russell and Sinclair saw in their own times a repetition of the pre-Civil War unrest. As homemade evolutionists and environmentalists, even when they were not economic determinists, they accepted this as the path to progress.

With their firm belief that they were contributing to the progress of society, the muckrakers might have been justified in considering themselves a constructive force on the basis of their criticism alone. Sweep away the forces which hindered or corrupted public opinion, the muckrakers were convinced, and the battle was half won. Even so, each of the journalists developed his own reform theories. G. K. Turner believed that organized business would free the nation from the combination of vice and boodle. C. P. Connolly sought methods by which the machinery of the law might function effectively in the public interest. Will Irwin believed that with a certain amount of public awakening the competitive processes would be an effective barrier to business excess. Alfred Henry Lewis, Burton J. Hendrick, and Ida Tarbell relied on competition but felt that somewhat more drastic action was necessary to make it function. Lewis favored any legislation that would end great fortunes, for he held that popular adulation of the rich had dulled the competitive individualism of the average citizen. Burton Hendrick felt that the states had the legal and legitimate right to regulate and require service from the corporations. Ida Tarbell believed that breaking the trust monopoly on transportation was essential, but that public scorn of unfair action was the best way to regain lost values.

Samuel Hopkins Adams and Thomas Lawson maintained that Wall Street lay at the heart of the trouble. They demanded that stock market gambling be prevented and that the government take steps to end the over-capitalization of industry which raised the cost of living. Ray Stannard Baker, David Graham Phillips, and Lincoln Steffens believed that certain key industries should be publicly owned and operated. Baker considered joining the Socialist Party but, while absorbing much of its ideology, he ended up by temporarily resting his faith in the pragmatism of La Folette's insurgent movement. Steffens and Phillips were also attracted by socialism but held back from Party membership. Charles Edward Russell came to believe that vast changes were needed in order to correct the evils of society. He and Upton Sinclair embraced socialism as the means by which society was to be rebuilt.

The writers of magazine exposés were basically moderates in most fields. They spoke as representatives of the middle classes of the nation's cities and towns. It would be difficult to apply Richard Hofstadter's thesis in the *Age of Reform*[8] to the muckrakers and maintain that they were led to reform as members of the old middle class which was being shaded by the rise of the trusts and the great fortunes. The muckrakers, perhaps apart from their class confreres, were at the peak of their professional power and mobility. On the whole, they came to the Progressive movement through the discovery of national corruption, rather than by conscious or unconscious comparison of their class or status position. As a group, they looked neither backward to an intensely democratic small America nor forward to a highly centralized nationalistic state. With the exception of Charles Edward Russell, they did not understand or attach any great importance to the agrarian unrest of the previous decades. Nor did they preach a doctrine of class warfare. There were stirrings of the latter phenomenon in the writings of Baker, Phillips, Russell, and Sinclair, but even they saw class conflict as a peaceful force working within the democratic framework. The socialism of Upton Sinclair and Charles Edward Russell was not extreme and contained only a limited amount of the Marxian paraphernalia. It was primarily a sense of frustration that led Russell into increasing radicalism in the last days before the outbreak of the First World War. In the main, the muckrakers believed that they did not believe that virtue resided solely in any one group in the society. They were for "the public," whose interests, however, always seemed to be typically middle class.

This is clearly shown in the attitude toward organized labor. Although all of these journalists at one time or another wrote on the subject of unions and the plight of the wage earner, they were usually without conclusions. They merely cautioned against violence and lamented unfair union practices. None saw labor as a counter-balancing group to aggregate wealth in a compromise society. On the other hand, only Burton Hendrick was openly hostile. The sins of labor seemed less menacing than those of capital, and there was much talk of "the public" whose interests had to be protected against both the unions and the trusts.

One theme that was almost completely absent from the writings of the muckrakers was a consideration of "big government." Hendrick alone dealt with it explicitly. He opposed centralized national power, but he did not believe that it threatened to become a reality. When the magazine crusaders pondered the role of the national government, they were concerned only with the privileges which might be given to business. For the most part, the non-socialists believed that the existing type of government would endure if it could be made responsive to the will of an informed people. To this end, the muckrakers offered enlightenment in their columns and called for such reforms as initiative, referendum, recall, direct primaries, and the popular election of Senators. One might suppose from the Socialists' talk of public operation for the common good, that a super-bureaucracy was in the making. However, they did not discuss this possibility. Although control of the national administration was to affect the revolution, Sinclair talked of his cooperative commonwealth as though it were a series of individual utopian colonies. Russell never dealt with the problem at all.

Probably the outstanding weakness in the philosophy of the muckrakers was their lack of a broad knowledge of economics. Although highlighting many evils, most of them did not understand the workings of the industrial and financial mechanisms. As George Mowry, the leading authority on this era, has pointed out, the Progressives tended to talk in "moral rather than economic terms."[9] This was surely true of the muckrakers. Whether or not it was a substitute for the middle class absence of a consciousness of class consciousness, they placed great emphasis upon the role of public-spirited altruism. However, if their outlook was moralistic because they believed that man could be made "good," the means was to pass laws to change the environment and conditions which made men "bad."

The strong point in the ideas of Samuel Hopkins Adams and Tom Lawson was their realization that there was much about the industrial machine which could not be controlled by public opinion and moral pressure. Having a better understanding of the financial organization of business, they explained why over-capitalization forced higher prices on the American consuming public. The muckrake-Socialists had the most detailed conception of how the economic mechanism worked. Charles Edward Russell cogently connected public buying power with industrial health, and he explained how over-capitalization and the drive for profits forced business to act in a way inimical to its own interests. The malignant force of "the surplus" held a central role in the analyses of Russell and Upton Sinclair. Their apocalyptic brand of economics, however, had the faults of its virtues. There is, perhaps something depressing and pessimistic about a social process—even when working toward the best of ends—which is not amenable to the control or direction of the men whom it is supposed to aid.

Most of the muckrakers were not looking backward. Perhaps, a few exponents of an anti-trust, competitive America, thought longingly of the days gone by. The vast majority of the others would have agreed with Lincoln Steffens when he attacked those who mistakenly believed that the nation could turn back the pages of history to the days of Thomas Jefferson or Andrew Jackson.[10] Will Irwin, who felt that the existing institutions were satisfactory, maintained that competition would work because it would adjust the new industrialism to the service of the common people. Steffens, Phillips, and Baker, as well as the muckrake-Socialists, were convinced that the forces of evolution were at work in human society. The Socialists saw a future of increasing progress and believed that trusts were an inevitable step in the movement toward a co-operative commonwealth. Others lauded the new industrialism and the good that might result from its enormous output. G. K. Turner, declining to blame big business for corruption, felt that it was bringing order to a chaotic competitive world. David Graham Phillips wrote the most enthusiastic message of praise in *The Reign of Gilt*. America, he explained proudly, was being emancipated by the machine. By raising the nation's standard of living, industry was working like science and education to break down prejudice and ignorance. By contributing to a new political fluidity, it would bring the end of the bosses and plutocracy.

Most of the journalists searched for hopeful signs of the growing productivity being applied to the service of the community. Burton Hendrick hailed the workers' villages of Gary, as well as the Carnegie and Rockefeller foundations, although the rest of the muckrakers strongly opposed anything that had the appearance of philanthropy or charity. Ida Tarbell was quick to seize upon the first encouraging instances of public-spiritedness on the part of the titans of industry. Steffens, with his interests in the techniques of leadership, relied upon the outstanding men of politics and business to bring the mass of citizens to a higher sense of community service. Many of the writers praised the scientific management theories of F. W. Taylor. Upton Sinclair alone raised a discordant note by demanding to know exactly how the greater profits were to be divided.[11]

Although concentrating on the central problems of society, the crusading journalists sought a more complete democracy in all parts of American life. Together with Russell, Tarbell, Baker and Sinclair, Phillips examined the role of the woman in the partnerships of marriage and national affairs. Turner and Steffens found the city a unique opportunity for experimentation in progressive democracy. As a group, the muckrakers had no agrarian prejudice against city or immigrant, even though there were strong strains of love for the land and nostalgia for the small town in the writing of Baker and

Phillips. Upton Sinclair alone displayed hatred for the life of the metropolis which he equated with plutocratic consumption and exploitation of the immigrant.

It would be difficult to maintain that the muckrakers followed at least some of their Progressive brethren along the paths of racism or Anglo-Saxon bias. Will Irwin was a little gullible on the subject of the Negro, but his failure to arrive at any solution to the West Coast prejudice was not based upon a belief in racial or cultural inferiority of the Oriental. Ray Stannard Baker's abandonment of his strident advocacy of Negro equalitarianism was in reality a retreat from socialism. Although he came to recommend a slower path, he did not give up his opposition to second-class citizenship for the Negro. Phillips and Russell were strongly critical of English society. Hendrick followed the liberal anthropology of Franz Boas in explaining varying ethnic stocks in terms of the plasticity of man responding to differences in environment. Lincoln Steffens, in writing of corruption in Philadelphia and Rhode Island, maintained that corrupt government was not ethnic, but American. Phillips hailed the immigrant as a strong force against aristocracy and tyranny. All of the muckrakers believed, with Charles Edward Russell, that any action which denied the "normal ties of sympathy and goodwill between men" exacted a cost too great for any nation to bear.[12]

The wielders of the muckrake exposed corruption in order that it might be corrected. Their analysis of national life probed deeply into the vast changes that had taken place during the previous half-century. Collectively they presented one of the first comprehensive descriptions of the business civilization that had become the ideal and the motive force of the American nation. With their criticism the muckrakers helped lay the groundwork of public concern which resulted in many of the reforms of the next half-century. In addition, these journalists had positive reform views to express and were able to do so in the popular magazines for more than a decade. They explained that the corruption which had become general in American life resulted from the privileges sought and obtained by the giant business enterprises that had emerged in the United States after the Civil War. The muckrakers did not reject the new industrialism and the dominant corporate form, but rather insisted that both be used for the public good.

The best illustration of the nature of the muckrakers' message can be found in a letter which Lincoln Steffens wrote to Theodore Roosevelt in the spring of 1907:

> I am not seeking proof of crime and dishonesty. . . . What I am after is the cause and the purpose and the methods by which our government, city, state and federal is made to represent not the common, but the special interests; the reason why it is so hard to do right in the U.S.; the secret of the power which makes it necessary for you, Mr. President, to fight to give us a "square deal." In brief, I want to . . . explain why it is that you have to force the Senate to pass a pure food bill or one providing for the regulation of railroads. . . .
>
> And please don't misunderstand me. . . . This is a point on which you, Mr. President, and I have never agreed. . . . I am looking upward to—an American Democracy. You ask men in office to be honest, I ask them to serve the people. . . .[13]

REFERENCES

CHAPTER 1

1. New York Bureau of National Literature, *A Compilation Of the Messages and Papers of the Presidents*, XII, 6645, 6647-48.

2. N. W. Ayer and Sons, *American Newspaper Annual*, (Philadelphia, Pa. 1901-1910).

3. Charles Edward Russell, *Bare Hands and Stone Walls* (New York, 1933), p. 134; Louis Filler, *Crusaders for American Liberalism*, 2nd. ed (Antioch, 1950), p. 57; Mark Sullivan, *The Education of an American* (New York, 1928), pp. 165-77; Alfred Henry Lewis, *Hearst's Magazine*, XXIV (1913), 344-45.

4. *McClure's*, XX (1903), 336.

5. Will Irwin, *The Making of a Reporter* (New York, 1942), p. 165; John A. Thayer, *Astir: A Publisher's Life Story* (Boston, 1910), pp. 249-86.

6. Walter Lippmann, *Drift and Mastery* (New York, 1914), p. 1.

7. Louis Filler, *Crusaders for American Liberalism*, p. 53.

8. Will Irwin, *Reporter*, pp. 92, 170-71; Isaac F. Marcosson, *David Graham Phillips and His Times* (New York, 1932), pp. 178-79, 280; C. E. Russell, *Bare Hands and Stone Walls*, pp. 143-44; Alfred Henry Lewis to Theodore Roosevelt, January [1907 ?] MS. Theodore Roosevelt Collection (Library of Congress, Washington).

9. C. E. Russell, *Bare Hands and Stone Walls*, pp. 193-94.

10. January 6, 1906, and January, 1909, MS. Ray Stannard Baker Collection (Library of Congress, Washington).

CHAPTER 2

1. *Atlantic Monthly*, LXXXV (1900), 784-94; *The Taskmasters* (New York, 1902).

2. *McClure's* XXVII (1906), 610-20; XXVIII (1907), 575-92; *Collier's*, XL (November 9, 1907), 13-14; (November 16, 1907), 17-18; *McClure's*, XXXIII (1909), 117-34; XXXV (1910), 97-108; XXXVIII (1912), 575-91.

3. *McClure's*, XXVIII (1907), 591, 685.

4. *Ibid.*, pp. 575-92; *McClure's*, XXXIII (1909), 117-34, 528-43; XXXIV (1909), 45-61; XXXV (1910), 346-48, 471-73; XXXVI (1910), 122; XLI (1913), 25-33; *Harper's*, LVII (June 21, 1913), 11.

5. *McClure's*, XXVIII (1907), 576.

6. *McClure's*, XXVII (1906), 619.

7. *McClure's*, XXXIV (1910), 339-54.

8. *McClure's*, XXXVI (1910), 2-24, 123-40; (1911), 334-52, 546-77; XXXVII (1911), 73-87, 185-202, 418-28; XL (1913), 25-35.

9. *Ibid.*, XXXVI, 17.

10. *Ibid.*, XXXVI, 345; XXXVII, 190.

CHAPTER 3

1. Quoted by Richard Hofstadter, *The American Political Tradition and the Men Who Made It* (New York, 1951), p. 176.

2. Charles Fairman, *Political Science Quarterly*, L (1935), 43.

3. *McClure's*, XXVII (1906), 346-61, 451-65, 629-39; XVIII (1906), 23-43, 198-210; XXIX (1907), 1-16, 214-28, 317-32; See also *Everybody's*, XXVI (1912), 152-55; Mark Sullivan, *The Education of An American* (New York, 1938), p. 202.

4. *McClure's*, XXVII, 452.

5. *Collier's*, XXXIX (May 11, 1907), 13-15; (May 18, 1907), 21-22; (May 25, 1907), 23; (June 22, 1907), 11-12; (June 29, 1907), 15-17, 28-29; (July 6, 1907), 11-12; (July 20, 1907), 13-14; (July 27, 1907), 13-14; XL (December 7, 1907), 19-20; (January 25, 1908), 11-12; XLVIII (October 14, 1911), 17, 31, 32; (December 23, 1911), 9-10; (January 13, 1912), 9-10.

6. *Collier's*, XXXIX (May 11, 1907), 13; XLVIII (December 23, 1911), 10.

7. *Collier's*, XLI (April 4, 1908), 13-14; (May 30, 1908), 26; (August 22, 1908), 16; XLII (January 9, 1909), 7; XLIII (April 3, 1909), 13-14; XLIV (January 8, 1910), 18; XLIX (August 31, 1912), 10-11; (September 14, 1912), 10-11, 32, 35; L (December 21, 1912), 12-13.

8. *Collier's*, XLIV (December 18, 1909), 8-9; (January 8,

1910), 18; XLV (April 2, 1910), 16-17; (April 9, 1910), 16-17, 28, 30; (July 16, 1910), 15; Cornelius C. Regier, *The Era of the Muckrakers* (Chapel Hill, 1932), pp. 115-16.

9. *Collier's*, XLII (April 3, 1909), 14; *Everybody's* XXVI (1912), 662-63.

10. *Collier's*, XLVIII (January 13, 1912), 9.

11. *Everybody's*, XXVI (1912), 150.

12. *Everybody's*, XXVI (1912), 146-60, 291-30, 439-53, 659-72; 827-41; XXVII (1912), 116-28; *Collier's*, XLII (February 20, 1909), 9.

CHAPTER 4

1. Louis Filler, "Alfred Henry Lewis and the Wolfville Tales," *New Mexico Quarterly Review*, XIII (1946), 35-47.

2. *The Verdict*, III (November 1, 1900), 1.

3. *The Boss and How He Came to Rule New York* (New York, 1903), p. 36; *Richard Croker* (New York, 1901); Kansas City *Star* (December 23, 1919), p. 4.

4. *Success*, VIII (1905), 169-71; *Human Life*, I (1905), 3; II (1906), 14-15; III (1906), 14-15; *Hearst's Magazine*, XXV (1914), 340-48. See also Lewis-Roosevelt correspondence, 1907-1908, Theodore Roosevelt Collection (Library of Congress, Washington).

5. *Cosmopolitan*, XXXVIII (1905), 666-672; XXXIX (1905), 312; XL (1906), 608-09, 645; XLV (1908), 621; *Human Life*, II (March, 1906), 14-15; IV (October, 1906), 19; *Hearst's Magazine*, XXV (1914), 340-48; *Success*, VIII (1905), 169-71; *World Today*, XXI (1911), 1330-32; (1912), 1687-94.

6. *Cosmopolitan*, XLII (1907), 293; XL (1906), 603-08.

7. *Cosmopolitan*, XL (1906), 609.

8. *Human Life*, VIII (March, 1909), 7.

9. Will Irwin, *The Making of a Reporter* (New York, 1942), pp. 137, 150.

10. *Collier's*. XL (September 28, 1907), 13-15; (October 12, 1907), 13-15; (October 19, 1907). 17-19; (October 16, 1907), 15-16; *Pearson's*, XXI (1909), 582-91; *The Making of a Reporter*, p. 159.

11. *American*, LXVII (1909), 564-75.

12. *Collier's*, XL (February 29, 1908), 10-12; (March 21, 1908), 13-14; (March 28, 1908), 13-14; (April 4, 1908), 16-18; (May 9, 1908). 9-11; (May 16, 1908), 9-10; XLI (August 15, 1908), 27-29; XLII (March 13, 1909), 27-28.

13. *Collier's*, XLI (July 11, 1908). 10-11, 23-26; XLVIII (January 6, 1912), 11-12; (January 13, 1912), 12-13.

14. *American*, LXVII (1909), 564.

15. *Collier's*, XLVI (January 21, 1911), 15-18; (February 4, 1911), 14-17; (February 18, 1911), 14-17; (March 4, 1911), 18-20; XLVII (April 1, 1911), 18-19; (April 22, 1911), 21-22; (May 6, 1911), 17-19; (May 27, 1911), 15-16; (June 3, 1911), 15-16; (June 17, 1911), 17-19; (July 1, 1911), 17-18; (July 8, 1911), 15-16; (July 22, 1911), 13; (July 29, 1911), 15-16.
16. *The Making of a Reporter*, p. 164.
17. *Harper's*, LXVIII (March 28, 1914), 10-12; *Collier's*, XLVI (March 4, 1911), 18-20.
18. *Collier's*, XLVII (July 8, 1911), 15.

CHAPTER 5
1. *Atlantic*, XCII (1903), 665-73.
2. *McClure's*, XXIV (1905), 563-64; XXVIII (1907), 307-21; XXXV (1910), 36-50, 373-87; XL (1913), 125-28.
3. *McClure's*, XXX (1908), 530-36, 671-72.
4. *McClure's*, XXVII (1906), 37-49, 156-70, 237-51, 401-12, 539-50, 659-71; XXVIII (1906), 61-73.
5. *McClure's*, XXX (1907), 33-48, 236-50; (1908), 322-38.
6. *McClure's*, XXII (1908), 57, 61-62; XXX (1908), 333-36; XXXIII (1909, 641-59; XXXVIII (1912), 501.
7. *McClure's*, XXX (1908), 530-36, 671-72; XXXVI (1911), 484-500; XXXVIII (1911), 217-31.
8. *McClure's*, XXXVII (1911), 234-48.
9. *McClure's*, XXXV (1910), 511-12; XXX (1908), 530, 673-74.
10. *McClure's*, XXXIX (1912), 561-80.
11. *McClure's*, XXXI (1908), 675.
12. *McClure's*, XL (1912), 170.
13. *McClure's*, XXXI (1908), 678; XXXVIII (1912), 414.
14. *McClure's*, XXXVII (1911), 441.
15. Reprinted as *The History of the Standard Oil Company* (New York, 1904), I, 21, 36-37, 159-60. See also David M. Chalmers, "Ida M. Tarbell," *Notable American Women, 1607-1950* (Radcliffe College).
16. *Ibid.*, II, 27, 211, 225, 267, 284-87.
17. *Ibid.*, I, 37.
18. *All in the Day's Work* (New York, 1939), p. 230.
19. *The History of the Standard Oil Company*, II, 229-30.
20. *Ibid.*, II, 27-277, 279-80, 283.
21. *Ibid.*, II, 77, 283-84.
22. M. C. Crawford, *Public Opinion*, XXXVIII (1905), 816; W. R. Linn, *Human Life*, II (March 1906), 24.
23. *The History of the Standard Oil Company*, II, 284; *Mc-*

Clure's, XXV (1905), 227, 229; XXVI (1906), 460; M. I. Macdonald, *Craftsman*, XIV (1908), 7-10.
24. *McClure's*, XXV (1905), 249, 393-94, 396-98.
25. *The History of the Standard Oil Company*, II, 292.
26. *American*, LXV (1908), 451-64; LXVII (1908), 29-41, 124-38.
27. *All in the Day's Work*, pp. 268-71.
28. Reprinted as *The Tariff in Our Times* (New York, 1911), 325-27, 358-64.

CHAPTER 6
1. *Collier's*, XXXVI (October 7, 1905), 14-15, 29; (October 28, 1905), 17-19; (November 18, 1905), 20-21; (December 2, 1905), 16-18; (January 13, 1906), 18-20; (February 17, 1906), 22-24, 26, 27; XXXVII (April 28, 1906), 16-18, 30; (July 14, 1906), 12-14, 22; (August 4, 1906), 14-16; (September 1, 1906), 16-18; XXXVIII (September 22, 1906), 16-18; (November 17, 1906), 17; XXXIX (June 8, 1907), 11-12; (August 3, 1907), 9-11; XL (October 12, 1907), 7-8; *Hampton's*, XXIV (1910), 234-42; *Collier's*, XLVIII (January 20, 1912), 11-12, 26-27; (February 17, 1912), 17-18; XLIX (May 11, 1912), 13-15; (June 22, 1912), 10-11. See also *Hamilton Alumni Review*, II (1937), 54-55; Will Irwin, *The Making of a Reporter* (New York, 1942), pp. 155-56.
2. *Collier's*, XLVIII (January 20, 1912), 26.
3. *Collier's*, XXXIX (August 3, 1907), 11.
4. *Hampton's*, XXIV (1910), 242.
5. *Ridgway's*, (October 6, 1906), pp. 4-5; (October 27, 1906), p. 6; (November 3, 1906), p. 8; (November 24, 1906), p. 9; (December 1, 1906), p. 9; (December 8, 1906), p. 9.
6. *Ibid.*, (October 6, 1906), pp. 4-5; (October 20, 1906), p. 6; (November 24, 1906), p. 12; (December 1, 1906), p. 9; *McClure's*, XXXI (1908), 246-47.
7. *Cosmopolitan*, XLIX (1910), 464-65.
8. *Frenzied Finance* (New York, 1905), vol. I [sic], reprinted from *Everybody's*, XII-XIV (1905-1906).
9. *Ibid.*, pp. 413-86; *Everybody's*, XIX (1906), 407-13; 545-49, 691-95; XV (1906), 549-53.
10. *Frenzied Finance*, pp. 179-81, 229-30, 290-93, 456, 479-80, 529, 551, 559; John A. Thayer, *Astir: Out of the Rut* (New York, 1912), pp. 254-55. See also *Success*, XI (1908), 146.
11. *Frenzied Finance*, pp. 476, 481-86, 546-47.
12. Frank Favant, "The Real Lawson," *Success*, X (1907), 663-67, 701, 703, 719, 722, 783-88, 819-22, 868-69; XI (1908),

23-25, 42, 71-73, 105-07; *The New York Times,* February 9, 1925, p. 19.

13. *Frenzied Finance,* pp. 35-36; *Everybody's,* XIV (1906), 691-96.

14. *Everybody's,* XVIII (1908), 288.

15. *Outlook,* XC (1908), 9-10; *Nation,* LXXXI (1905), 496-97; *Collier's,* XXXV (April 22, 1905), 22, 25, 27; (May 20, 1905), 23, 25.

16. Frank Fayant, *op. cit.,* pp. 819-22, 868-69.

17. *The Deluge* (Indianapolis, 1905), p. 244. See also Fayant, *op. cit.,* p. 785.

18. *New England Monthly,* n.s. XXXIX (1909), 390-96; *Everybody's,* XV (1906), 65-74, 204-08; XVII (1907), 856-58.

19. *Everybody's,* XIV (1906), 691-92; XV (1906), 714-18; XVIII (1908), 287-88, 48a-x.

20. *Nation,* LXXXI (1905), 497; *Outlook,* XC (1908), 9; *Collier's,* XXXV (April 22, 1905), 27. See also *Arena,* XXXIV (1905), 304.

21. *Everybody's,* XV (1906), 714-15; Fayant, *op. cit.,* X, 171.

22. *Everybody's,* XVIII (1908), 287-88.

23. *Everybody's,* XXVII (1912), 472a-t, 601-16, 777-92; XXX-VIII (1913) 89-104, 201-14, 404-15, 550-60, 649-55, 843-52; XXIX (1913), 60-61.

24. *Ibid.,* XXVII, 606-08.

25. *Ibid.,* XXVII, 601-04, 605-08, 616.

26. *Ibid.,* XXVIII, 654; XXIX, 61; *The New York Times,* February 18, 1912.

CHAPTER 7

1. *Our New Prosperity* (New York, 1900), pp. 17-20; *Seen in Germany* (New York, 1901); *McClure's,* XVIII (1901), 3-13.

2. *McClure's,* XX (1903), 323-36; XXI (1903), 451-63; XXII (1903), 30-43, 194-97; XXII (1904), 368-78; XXIII (1904), 43-57; 279-92; XXIV (1904), 41-52. See also "Trade Union Against Trust," unpublished MS., and untitled lecture given at Pomona College, California, March 4, 1903, MS Ray Stannard Baker Collection (Library of Congress, Washington).

3. *McClure's,* XXII (1903), 195-97.

4. Letters, Theodore Roosevelt to Baker, October 21, 1903; Baker to his father, January 31, 1904, March 27, 1904, January 29, 1905. Baker MS.

5. Notebook C, pp. 45, 63-64, 70-78; Notebook I, pp. 137, 140, Baker MS.

6. *McClure's,* XXVI (1905), 47-59, 179-94, 318-31, 398-411,

534-49, 672-74; XXVII (1906), 131-45; *Collier's*, XXXVII (June 9, 1906), 19, 20, 22.

7. Letters, W. Z. Ripley to Baker, January 4, 1906; Theodore Roosevelt to Baker, September 13, 1905; Baker to Roosevelt, November 11, 1905, Baker MS. See also *American Chronicle* (New York, 1945), 194-95, 198-200.

8. Notebook C, p. 157, Baker MS.

9. *Ibid.*, pp. 70-77, 99-100, 119, 121.

10. *Ibid.*, pp. 125-27; Notebook I, pp. 36-38, 66-67, 76, 77.

11. Notebook I, pp. 111-12, Baker MS.

12. Notebook J, pp. 128-33, Baker MS.

13. *Ibid.*, pp. 107-28.

14. *Ibid.*, pp. 134, 140.

15. Letter, Baker to Roosevelt, June 8, 1908, Baker MS.

16. *McClure's*, XXIV (1905), 451-609; unpublished lecture given at Harvard University, January 23, 1905; Los Angeles *Times* and San Diego *Union*, April 16, 1906. Baker MS.

17. *Following the Color Line* (New York, 1908), p. 269. See also letter, Theodore Roosevelt to Baker, June 3, 1908; Notebook I, pp. 165-66, Baker MS.

18. See David Chalmers, "Ray Stannard Baker's Search for Reform," *Journal of the History of Ideas*, XIX (1958), 422-34.

19. Notebook J, p. 139, Baker MS.

20. *The Spiritual Unrest* (New York, 1910), reprinted from *American*, LXVII-LXIX (1909).

21. October 31, 1909, Baker MS.

22. Letter, Baker to Roosevelt, written October 5, 1910, but not sent; Notebook K, pp. 151-73. Baker MS.

23. *American*, LXIX (1910), 435-48, 579-87; LXX (1910), 147-54, 370-71; LXXI (1910), 6.

24. *American*, LXXII (1911), 61. See also Belle and Fola La Follette, *Robert M. La Follette* (New York, 1953), pp. 341, 363-65; 1911-1912, Baker MS.

CHAPTER 8

1. Charles Edward Russell, *Bare Hands and Stone Walls* (New York, 1933), p. 193; Lincoln Steffens, *The Autobiography of Lincoln Steffens* (New York, 1931), p. 434; *The Letters of Lincoln Steffens*, Ella Winter and Granville Hicks, eds. (New York, 1938), I, 203.

2. Ida Tarbell, *All in the Day's Work* (New York, 1939), p. 298.

3. *Ainslee's* VIII (1901), 213-20; *The Autobiography of Lincoln Steffens*, pp. 253-54, 266-84.

4. Reprinted as *The Shame of the Cities* (New York, 1904), p. 5.

5. *Ibid.*, pp. 29-62, 101-43; Reprinted as *The Struggle For Self-Government* (New York, 1906), 3-38, 79-119, 161-208; *McClure's*, XXI (1903), 419-25; *American*, LXIII (1906), 20.

6. *The Upbuilders* (New York, 1909), p. 278; *American*, LXX (1910), 744-46; *Everybody's*, XX (1909), 57-62; XXV (1911), 796-99.

7. *Metropolitan*, XXXIX (February, 1914), 32; (March, 1914), 12-13, 68; (April, 1914), 18-19, 58-59, 62; XL (May, 1914), 33-34, 51-54.

8. *McClure's*, XL (1914), 79-84, 188-208; *The Struggle for Self-Government*, pp. 38-39; *The Upbuilders*, p. 8. See also David Graham Phillips' definition in "The Treason of the Senate."

9. Irving Stone, *Clarence Darrow for the Defense*, Chapter VIII.

10. *American*, LXVI (1908), 127-30; *Everybody's*, XVIII (1908), 723-36,a. 58; XIX (1909), 3-15; XXIII (1910), 391-98, 449-60, 646-56, 813-25; XXIV (1911), 217-29, 455-56; Steffens to Theodore Roosevelt, June 9, 1908. MS. Lincoln Steffens Collection (Columbia University, New York).

11. *Everybody's*, XVIII (1908), 723, XIX (1908), 12.

12. *Everybody's*, XIX (1908), 455-69.

13. *Everybody's*, XXIII (1910), 813-25.

14. *The Letters of Lincoln Steffens*, I, 237, 298-99; *American*, LXIII (1906), 3-23; LXV (1907), 26-40.

15. *Saturday Evening Post*, CLXXV (June 6, 1903), 3.

16. *The Second Generation* (New York, 1907), p. 15.

17. *The Hungry Heart* (New York, 1909); *The Husband's Story* (New York, 1910); *The Grain of Dust* (New York, 1910); *The Price She Paid* (New York, 1912); *The Worth of a Woman* (New York, 1908); *Delinquent*, LXXVII (1911), 265-66; *Cosmopolitan*. L (1911), 419-25.

18. *The Cost* (Indianapolis, 1904); *The Plum Tree* (Indianapolis, 1905); *The Light Fingered Gentry* (New York, 1907).

19. *Cosmopolitan*, XL (1906), 477-78, 487-502, 628-38; XLI (1906), 3-12, 123-32, 267-76, 368-77, 525-35, 627-36; XLII (1906), 77-84.

20. C. E. Russell, *Bare Hands and Stone Walls*, 143-45; I. F. Marcosson, *David Graham Phillips and His Times* (New York, 1932), pp. 238-41; *The Lives of Eighteen from Princeton*, Williard Thorp, ed. (Princeton, 1946), p. 323.

21. *Cosmopolitan*, XXXVIII (1904), 123-30; XL (1906), 603-10; *Saturday Evening Post*, CLXXVI (September 19, 1903), 10; *Reader*, V (1905), 166-75; *Arena*, XXXV (1906), 258-64.

22. *Cosmopolitan*, XLI (1906), 525; *Arena*, XLI (1909), 17-19.

References   125

23. *The Second Generation*, p. 203. See also *George Helm* (New York, 1912), pp. 178-80.

24. Louis Filler, "Murder in Gramercy Park," *Antioch Review*, VI (1946), 495-508.

25. *The Conflict* (New York, 1912), p. 62.

CHAPTER 9

1. Upton Sinclair, *American Outpost* (New York, 1932); Floyd Dell, *Upton Sinclair* (New York, 1927); John Chamberlain, *Farewell to Reform* (New York, 1932), pp. 179-82; *Cosmopolitan*, XLI (1906), 591-93.

2. Dell, *op. cit.*, pp. 97-99.

3. *Independent*, LVII (1904), 1149; *Collier's* XXXIV (October 8, 1904), 23-25.

4. *Appeal to Reason*, September 17, 1904, p. 1.

5. *Collier's*, XXXIV (October 8, 1904), 22; (October 29, 1904), 10-12.

6. *Collier's*, XXXIV (November 26, 1904), 23; *The Jungle* (New York, 1906), pp. 399-400.

7. *Ibid.*, pp. 377, 382, 411-13.

8. *Ibid.*, pp. 401, 406, 407; *The Industrial Republic* (New York, 1907), p. 283.

9. *Independent*, LX (1906), 1404-07; LXII (1907), 306-13; *American*, LXIV (1907), 329; *The Industrial Republic*, pp. 280-83.

10. *Cosmopolitan*, XLI (1906), 591-93; *Current Literature*, XLI (1906), 164; *Everybody's*, XIV (1906), 608-16; *Human Life*, III (September 1906), 5.

11. *Independent*, LX (1906), 1129-33; *Everybody's*, XIV (1906), 608-16; *Arena*, XXXVI (1906), 66-72; *Collier's*, XXXVI (1906), 24; XXXVII (1906), 24, 26; *American Outpost*, p. 167.

12. *Ibid.*, pp. 173-75; *The Brass Check—A Study of American Journalism* (Pasadena, California, 1919); *Independent*, LXII (1907), 312-13.

13. *The Industrial Republic*, pp. 11, 47.

14. *Collier's*, XXXIV (October 19, 1904), 12; *The Jungle*, p. 375; *The Industrial Republic*, pp. x-xi, 200-05.

15. *Independent*, LXV (1908), 519.

16. *Bare Hands and Stone Walls* (New York, 1933), p. 193.

17. *Ibid.*, pp. 1-45; *A Pioneer Editor in Early Iowa* (D.C., 1941); *Human Life*, VIII (December 1908), 11-12; Caro Lloyd, *Henry Demarest Lloyd* (New York, 1912), pp. vi-vii.

18. *Bare Hands and Stone Walls*, pp. 38, 42, 58-59, 78-96, 130; *These Shifting Scenes* (New York, 1914), pp. 39-40; *Harper's*, XLVIII (1904), 790-92; *Ridgway's*, I (1906), 9-11.

19. *The Greatest Trust in the World* (New York, 1905), pp. 1-3, 89, reprinted from *Everybody's*, XII-XIII (1905). See also *Lawless Wealth* (New York, 1908), pp. 281-88, reprinted from *Everybody's*, XVII-XVIII (1908).

20. *Cosmopolitan*, XLII (1907), 454.

21. *The Uprising of the Many* (New York, 1907), p. xiii, reprinted from *Everybody's*, XIII-XVI (1905-1907).

22. *The Uprising of the Many*, p. 358; *Wilshire's*, X (November 1906), 9, 11; *Cosmopolitan*, XLII (1907), 271-79.

23. *Why I Am a Socialist* (New York, 1910), p. 154; *Human Life*, VIII (December 1908), 11.

24. *Hearst's*, XXII (1912), 1734; *Hampton's*, XXII (1909), 124.

25. *Why I am a Socialist*, pp. 126, 128-33, 135, 137, 138, Ch. VIII.

26. *Doing Us Good and Plenty*. p. 156.

27. *Cosmopolitan*, XLIX (1910), 284.

28. *Business The Heart of the Nation* (New York, 1911), pp. 106-08, 175, reprinted from *Success*, XII-XIII (1909-1910).

29. *Success*, XII (1909), 5-9, 80-82, 119-21, 220-21, 263-67.

30. *Hampton's*, XXII (1909), 119-26; XXVII (1912), 752-63; *Business The Heart of the Nation*, pp. 275, 278; *Doing Us Good and Plenty*, pp. 171-72.

31. *International Socialist Review* (March, 1912), p. 457; *Success*, XIII (1910), 569-72. See also XXVII (1912), 752-53; *Cosmopolitan*, LII (1912), 468.

32. *Doing Us Good and Plenty*, pp. 44-81, 127; *Pearson's*, XXI (1914), 473-88; XXII (1914), 18-31; 306-15; *These Shifting Scenes*, pp. 73-75; 291-311; *The Story of Wendell Phillips* (Chicago, 1914), pp. 21-24, 48.

33. *Doing Us Good and Plenty*, pp. 171-72.

CHAPTER 10

1. Lincoln Steffens, *The Autobiography of Lincoln Steffens* (New York, 1931), Ch. XXXIII.

2. David Chalmers, "The Muckrakers and the Growth of Corporate Power," *American Journal of Economics and Sociology*, 18 (April, 1959), 295-311.

3. C. E. Russell, *Lawless Wealth* (New York, 1908), pp. 281-88; Upton Sinclair, *Independent*, LXV (1908), 517-19; Thomas Lawson, *Everybody's*, XV (1906), 204-08; A. H. Lewis, *Hearst's Magazine*, XXIV (1913), 344-45, and *Human Life*, I (June, 1906), 20; Ida Tarbell, *All in the Day's Work* (New York, 1939), pp. 242, 280-81; C. E. Russell, *Bare Hands and Stone Walls* (New York, 1933), pp. 143-44.

4. *Everybody's* XVIII (1908), 723-36, a. 58.

5. Notebook C, p. 45, MS. Ray Stannard Baker Collection (Library of Congress, Washington).

6. *American*, LXVII (1909), 564.

7. *The Upbuilders* (New York, 1909), pp. 98-99.

8. Richard Hofstadter, *The Age of Reform: From Bryan to FDR* (New York, 1955), Chs. 4-5.

9. George E. Mowry, *The Era of Theodore Roosevelt, 1900-1912* (New York, 1958), pp. 100-101.

10. *Everybody's*, XIX (1908), 15.

11. *American*, LXXI (1911), 564; *McClure's*, XLI (1912), 50-59; *American*, LXXVIII (October, 1914), 16-17; (November, 1914), 11-17; (December, 1914), 24-29; *American*, LXXII (1911), 243-44.

12. *Cosmopolitan*, XLII (1907), 455.

13. Letter, Lincoln Steffens to Theodore Roosevelt, March 6, 1907, MS. Lincoln Steffens Collection (Columbia University Library, New York).